GROWTH
of
Adolescence
A Guide for Teens and Parents

W. Luke Huang, M.D., M.B.A.

CONTENTS

Dedication

❖

To my wife
Susan Huang
From whom I learn love and understanding

Foreword

by **Rev. Felix Liu**, PhD.
President, Logos Evangelical Seminary
El Monte, California

s a pastor, I often hear parents, either on the phone or in person, talking about not knowing how to deal with the teenager at home. Parents often expect advisors at church to undertake about these young people at this rebellious stage. The parents are at their wit's end. Kids don't tell parents about many things, and they listen to their friends more than to their parents. The problem is worse, if they are "bad friends". Because church advisors are closer in age to teens have often gone through the same period, and care about them with the love of Christ, it is easier for them to gain these young people's trust. Consequently, they listen to advisors more than to their parents. Therefore, parents often seek help for their teenage sons and daughters through church advisors.

We are grateful that in the Chinese immigrant society of North America, churches have set up fellowships for this age group due to this kind of need. At the church where I am pasturing, there are English junior high and high school groups as well as Mandarin/Taiwanese junior high and high school groups, a total of approximately 120 people coming and going almost every Friday night at church. About twelve to thirteen college graduates and seminary students are advisors, ministering them with the love of God and the word of God. Sometimes we also arrange a parent-child conference night to promote understanding and dialogue between the teens and their parents.

The author of this book is an elder of the Evangelical Formosan Church of Orange County as well as a pediatrician. He has helped countless parents with his compassion, having led his own son and daughter through their adolescent periods. He often speaks on such topics, and this book is the product of counseling teenagers and their parents based on many years of practical experiences. With the triple identity of being a pediatrician, a father of a son and a daughter, and an adolescent expert, he writes this book focusing on families living in the North American culture.

If you are a teenager, this book is suitable for you to read. It will help you understand yourself, getting to know the growth and development of your own body, soul and spirit. There is much advice in this book, which will help you achieve healthy growth and development, especially the teaching on life in North American society in terms of interpersonal relationships, managing work, friendships and academic life.

If you are a parent, this book is suitable for you to read. It will help you understand your children, getting to know what they are thinking and the impact they encounter in this strange culture. The advice to all parents in this book will help you become a wiser parent, more understandable to raise your precious children successfully or a culture very different from the one you know.

If you are already an advisor to the youth, or you are preparing to become one, or you would like to help the young people around you, this book will help you understand the problems teenagers and their parents run into in North American society and equip you to help them. Much advice of the author is the product of years of research and helping these two groups of people based on practical experiences. And I believe it will help you accomplish this challenging ministry.

May this book be accepted and blessed by the hand of God in order to help many young people, their parents and their advisors.

Foreword

by Rev. Susan Chou, D.Min.

Senior Pastor, Evangelical Formosan Church
of Orange County

A dolescence is a period that everyone has to go through in the process of growing up. And during this period, they [teenagers] are changing, growing, knowing themselves, seeking the true self in order to answer the question: "Who am I?"

In this phase of growth, they have much confusion, fear, suspicion, and all kinds of stress in their heart, which is so difficult for them to bear that they behave differently from before. Many parents are not ready at all to understand their children and to help them endure this period that they might otherwise be successfully transformed and become mature youth who know themselves, affirm themselves and accept themselves.

I have seen some teenagers who received appropriate help from their parents. Because these parents not only tried to be their parents but also be their friends, these teenagers did not become people who rebelled against their parents, tradition and environment at this phase of development.

God entrusts children to parents as stewards who can help build up their character, personality, value and self-image. More importantly, parents are to help them know the God who created them so that in their course of life they may have a God in the highest to guide them, strengthen them, guard them and perfect them.

Dr. W. Luke Huang has always been a good co-worker of mine ever since I came to plant the Evangelical Formosan Church of Orange County. As a pediatrician, he has had much contact with many parents. Because of his care and compassion toward people, parents have quite naturally told him the difficulty of parenting and asked of his advice.

I believe due to such a need, he has spent much effort to research and study adolescent psychology. From a physician's point of view on the physiological changes during adolescence, and as a God-loving Christian with much effort in personal evangelism at church, he writes about the needs of adolescent transition from the three perspectives of spirit, soul and body.

This book will help parents understand their teenage sons and daughters. It will also help them prepare their hearts to welcome their children into adolescence and to accompany them during this difficult period that it might become the most wonderful years.

May God bless this book to help many people.

Foreword

by John Mace, M.D.
Professor and Chairman
Department of Pediatrics
Loma Linda University School of Medicine
Loma Linda, California

I have known Luke Huang for more than 25 years. During this time he has faithfully driven on a regular basis more than 50 miles each way to voluntarily teach the pediatric residents and medical students in the Pediatric Teaching Office. I have come to admire him for his patience, teaching skills, gentleness, and godly character.

His gentleness, kindness, knowledge, and obvious contentment not only make him a favorite teacher, but also, more importantly, reflect the joy and peace that is obvious in Christ's followers. This book, first written in Chinese for Chinese Christians, is now being published in English. While intended primarily for Chinese Americans, it will be of great value to Christians of any race or ethnic group. It is a book that is written for both parents and teenagers.

All 20 chapters are not only full of useful information, but contain many helpful suggestions of ways to deal with problems. The questions asked at the end of many chapters will provide thoughtful solutions to ways of handling problems before they arise.

Parents of teenagers as well as teenagers themselves will find this book to be not only informative, but also a useful guide to living in harmony with each other. Importantly, this book is based on biblical principles. These principles are timeless and always appropriate for any era, past, present, or future. The application of these principles to one's life will not only improves the relationship between teenagers and parents, but will also improve your walk with God. It is my pleasure to recommend this book to you.

Acknowledgements

henever I work in my medical office or meet with friends, I usually see or hear about confrontations between parents and their teenagers; and I can sense the pain of the parents and the helplessness of the teenagers. In reality, they really try to please each other, but the attempt usually fails in that there is a barrier that just cannot be broken. Have you had a similar experience before?

Parents, do you remember when we were back in our teenager years? We also caused pain for our parents. Now that we have become parents, we are also going through pain caused by our own teenagers. This "growing pain" is usually caused by the lack of mental preparation, experience, and understanding by parents. On the other side, teenagers are affected by the change in their hormones, the speedy development of their mind, spirit and body. In addition, society and peer pressure cause them to feel helpless, confused, and without direction. The lack of understanding between parents and teenagers then leads them to grow apart.

Praise the Lord! When I was struggling as a teenager, He gave me a new life. He loved me, accepted me, lets me enjoy the loves in life, and led me through the stormy times of my teenager years. Because of this love, I had the power to face tomorrow. When I look back on the road I have traveled, besides thanking my parents for their understanding, I also thank the Lord for His unconditional and everlasting love. It is He who gave me a new life.

Love gives people hope. Love gives strength to the parents and teenagers to continue. From the encouragement of patients, friends, and brothers and sisters in church over the years, I was able to write this book to share my knowledge about the growth of teenagers. I hope this book can be used as a guide for both parents and teenagers.

I would like to thank Mr. and Mrs. Paul Wang and Mr. and Mrs. Jack Lin for their continuing encouragement; to thank Dr. James Huang for his tremendous help, Dr. Joseph Chen for his invaluable input as an expert in teenagers' problems as well as Mr. And Mrs. King Wang's for their review of the book. I would also like to thank the publisher, EFCCC, ex- director, Rev. Tsai, my coordinator, Miss Julie Chuang, Mrs. Su and Mrs. Sau-Chun Tsuei for their corrections to the manuscript. I would like to give my special appreciation to professional writer, Mrs. Beverly Cook for her input. They are the ones who made this book possible.

I would like to thank Mr. and Mrs. Hendrix Tzoa for their financial contributions. I would also like to thank Dr. Felix Liu, Dr.

Susan Chou, and Dr. John Mace for the prefaces as well as many scientists, doctors and pastors for their recommendations of the book. Finally I would like to give thank to you, my readers, for your dedication to read this book.

Ultimately, I would like to give gratitude to the Lord for His grace. Because of His boundless love, He has called many angels of love in this world so our lives would be more beautiful and meaningful. I prayed to the Lord that He could use this book to assist parents and teenagers. May all the glories be given to Him.

W. Luke Huang, M.D., M.B.A.

1

Introduction

To Parents:

When "adolescence" is mentioned, most parents recall mixed feelings during this crucial time of great physical and emotional upheaval. Many may remember those days struggling with issues such as sexual desires versus guilt, confidence versus doubt, and acceptance versus rejection. Many often recall those terrifying days of asking and going on "dates" and of wondering whether the object of one's affections reciprocates the same feelings. This is also a period in which parental attitudes and roles change towards the adolescent from child to young adult.

Often conjuring up these memories brings many parents an unwillingness to share their adolescence with their children; however, our children need reassurance and guidance during this tumultuous life-changing stage. It would be a pity if lessons learned from this crucial time were not passed to our offspring. Through our guidance, children will gain comfort and encouragement as they go through tough times of fear, worry, failure, and disappointment. They may benefit from our wisdom gained from similar experiences. Many parents have expressed helplessness in counseling their children, especially when facing criticism from their adolescent for being "old fashioned."

This book is intended for parents with adolescent young adults who live at home. I hope that these shared experiences will provide many parents ideas of how to resolve many difficult situations.

To Adolescents Adults:

Congratulations to you all! You are slowly evolving from a child who is dependent upon parents to a self-sufficient person. You are entering into a new passage of life filled with newly found feelings from the physical, emotional, and intellectual, and spiritual aspects of your life. Due to these changes, you will undoubtedly question your perceptions, morals, and lifestyle. You will look at people and things in a new light. There will be times when you think that your parents, friends, and relatives do not totally understand or care about you. You might also believe that they only see you as a child. You might even hope to run away in order to gain independent and autonomy.

In reality, adolescence is a period during which drastic changes occurs. It is a prelude to maturity towards adulthood. Adolescence can be described on three levels: the physiological, emotional, and the spiritual. Despite the upheaval, adolescence is the healthiest period in life. You will face a physical growth spurt, affirmation of your personality and sexual orientation, development of personal, social, and cultural interrelationships, and the pursuit of spiritual direction.

Our society is facing the breakdown of the family unit:

According to statistics, one fourth of adolescents between ten and fifteen will suffer from learning, behavioral, and emotional disabilities. Although this is the healthiest period in life, between fifteen(15%) to nineteen percent(19%) of adolescents die from car accidents, murder, or suicide. Death resulting from AIDS ranks sixth among fifteen to twenty-four year olds. Drug abuse among adolescence is the fastest growing group as well as alcohol consumption. Sexually transmitted diseases such as herpes, gonorrhea, and syphilis have been increased 170% within the past twenty years. Premarital/teen pregnancy, abortion, and suicide are also on the rise.

This book describes the changes that take place during adolescence to help you understand this crucial passage in life. I urge adolescent adults and parents to share their thoughts and concerns in order to strengthen the family bond. May this help alleviate many fears as you face these changes?

2

Physiological Growth

I. As A Female Adolescent, I Am Filled With Anxiety

I am scared of the changes in my body.

The first year after my birth is when the primary growth spurt occurs. Around the ages of eight to ten years, the second growth spurt begins. Not only does the physical body change in terms of shape and weight; it is during this time when emotions, feelings, spirituality, intelligence, and sex organs all develop at an astounding speed. I understand that in general, girls physically develop two years earlier than boys.

As a result, girls often notice that we are taller than the boys in our class during this time period. We often discover that a soft layer of fat begins to accumulate which results in shaping our hips, breasts, and legs. Physiologically, a developing girl's pelvis also widens in order to accommodate childbirth. Shoulders broaden and swell one after the other. My breasts will grow and become tender. Within a year, pubic hair begins to grow. I rest assured though that, this is all part of God's plan in transforming a girl to a woman.

I begin to menstruate and it shocks me.

Within three years of developing breasts and hips, my menstruation often begins with abdominal discomfort. This is a normal process in which blood and tissues are released from the uterus. During the first couple of years of menstruation, no egg will be expelled from the ovaries. Once an egg is released from the ovaries, hormones such as progesterone will stimulate the uterus to contract and begin menstruation. Occasionally, dizziness, nausea, vomiting, and backache will occur. I was told not to worry or be fearful because these symptoms may be relieved through rest, diet, heat, and pain medication.

Menstruation usually begins by the age of fourteen; otherwise, you must check with a medical doctor for possible health problems. Menstruation is the beginning of womanhood, which God designed and created.

Pimples: Come to visit and stay.

Soon after menstruation, I begin to have body odor. Hair begins to grow under my armpits, legs, and pubic areas. Often, many young girls secretly shave their body hair. Pimples, an unwelcome guest, often appear on the face, chest, and back at the most stressful of times.

This is a time in which many girls lose their self-image and self-esteem because pimples and other physiological changes may alter the childhood perception of being pretty to ugly.

As a result of these many changes, many adolescent women become depressed and afraid to meet people, even to the point of barricading themselves within the home. Although this is an awkward time, the body will slowly adjust to reveal the beauty within.

My appetite increased, I'm sleepy, and lethargic.

During adolescence, appetites increase significantly. The adolescent body will also require more sleep, which is a normal phenomenon. Body growth occurs during sleep. As a result, female teens seem to be constantly hungry while simultaneously worrying about becoming obese. Sometimes this results in a cycle of snacking, sleeping, and dieting. This inconsistency often results in weight gain. Girls must pay even closer attention to our nourishment since we may be prone to iron deficiency anemia due to our menstruation.

Because my body has an increased need for sleep, I often feel lethargic. Unfortunately, many teachers assign more homework as well as increase the difficulty during this time because I am becoming more intellectually developed as well. As a result, however, many young developing adults feel overwhelmed by all of these changes—whether from stress, school or menstruation.

Often, girls feel that parents or siblings are disgusted with them. Sometimes, these girls feel like they are all alone and that parents and siblings do not understand.

After a period of physiological adjustment, usually five years after the beginning of menstruation, the female growth spurt slows. This is when many once awkward and insecure adolescent girls turn into beautiful young ladies. The ugly duckling has become a swan, just as God planned.

II. As A Male Adolescent I Am Very Clumsy

I wish people would not know my physiological secrets.

I am a late bloomer since I am two years behind girls. When I was between ten to twelve years old, my appetite suddenly grows. All of the food in the refrigerator cannot fill me up. My mother is greatly surprised to find my slim body lengthening as well as an increase in my weight. My shoulders broaden and my muscles grow taut. I have increased strength.

Soon, I outgrow the adolescent girl next door. But like her, I'm lethargic all of the time. I'm always "Late to bed, late to rise". I'm sometimes careless while playing ball in which I dent the garage door in which my parents end up scolding me.

I do not have as much fat under my skin as the girls. My pelvis does not grow as wide, either. God knows that my body is not suited to carry a child for nine months. When I take my bath, I discover that my testicles are bigger and my scrotum seems bloated. A year later, my penis grows longer and larger. Soon, I noticed that my pubic hair grows becoming thicker and thicker. I dare not to take baths with my little brother any more. I do not want him to know my physiological secrets. I want privacy. After all, I am all grown up and do not want to share everything with my brother, and parents.

Two years later, hair grows under my armpits. My body odor becomes strong. I have to use deodorant to hide the foul odor before I see people. My voice slowly begins to become hoarse and can't sing in choir anymore. My Adam's apple appears. The hair on my face and body is more noticeable. How embarrassing! I have to shave everyday. My body continues to grow and I often feel like a giant. Luckily by fifteen and sixteen, my body slows, but I noticed that my temper has worsened. I can't help feeling so frustrated and unable to vent my stress. About eighteen or twenty, my body stops to grow, but I have a hard time controlling my anger. So, I pour out my problems to my parents figuring that they are my closest relatives who can help me. But, guess what? They end up getting mad at me. I should have known better.

Wet dreams and masturbation make me uneasy.

One thing that terrifies me is that during my sleep some clear fluid ejaculates from my penis. I asked my big brother about it in which he told me not to worry. He called this a "wet dream". Later on, I learned that this is perfectly normal from a medical point of view. Almost every boy will experience it. I don't need to worry about it. It is a means of excreting the extra liquid produced by the body, especially my testicles. It does not mean that I am ill, except that at times I cannot control myself but have strange sexual fantasies. When I play my penis, the same thing happens every time. I feel excited at first, but I panic wondering if I have a serious medical condition.

29

Later, when my mother knows that I have the habit of masturbation and wet dreams, she takes me to see a doctor. My doctor tells me after giving me thorough physical and laboratory examinations that masturbation is a situation that all adolescents face. Approximately sixty to eighty percent (60-80%) of male adolescents and forty percent (40%) of female adolescents have these masturbation experiences. Many magazine and newspaper articles describe that masturbation will lead to sterility, body weakness, lethargy, and even insanity! I ask my doctor about what I have read and heard. He tells me that there is no medical basis to the claims.

However, if masturbation is very frequent, it may be caused by an emotional problem, which needs medical attention. I ask my Christian doctor what is the Christian view of masturbation. He says that while the Bible does not mention masturbation, there are many arguments surrounding it. My doctor encourages me not to get into the habit of doing it, but he says that I should not feel guilty about my masturbation experience either.

My doctor tells me that some adolescents feel very guilty about masturbation, yet they cannot refrain from it. His advice is to tell God about it and ask for His guidance since we can trust God cares for us even with difficult situations.

Annoying pimple make me looks for secret cures.

When all the physical changes are making my life uneasy, pimples further add to my misery. I wash, scrub, and squeeze them, which does not help, but makes things worse. Now, my face looks like a map full of holes. I do not feel like seeing anyone anymore. Luckily, I have found some secret cures, which give me a new lease on life. If you want to know these secret cures, please refer to chapter 16 of this book.

I have learned a great deal during these eight years of adolescence. I used to look into the mirror and be very critical of myself. I thought my nose was too small or flat. There was no perfect part on my body. I was ashamed of myself. Now, after these years, I am quite pleased with the body that God has provided for me. When I see other adolescents criticizing their bodies, I am thankful for what God has provided a nice suitable physique for me.

My doctor suggests that because of the enormous metabolic increments necessary for growth spurt, activity, and emotional stress during adolescence. I should pay great attention to have a balanced daily diet, which has 2500-3500 calories composed of fifteen percent (15%) of protein (90-100 gram), and 1,000-1,500 mg of Calcium for tremendous stress of protein and calcium storage and absorption. I also need to increase the intake of iron and other vitamins to avoid anemia.

3

Emotional Growth of Males and Females

There are three stages of emotional growth, in which each stage has special characteristics.

I. Early Adolescence- when I was eleven to fourteen years old, I loved to challenge authority.

I have always been a good obedient child. I was always proud of my parents and regarded them as my heros. But for reasons, which I cannot explain, I started to feel detached from my parents around the time when I was in fifth or sixth grade. I was no longer interested in hanging out with my parents. Sometimes, I would easily lose my temper around them. I readily challenged my parents' authority over everything.

If they would say something which I perceived as unpleasant or if they would raise their voice when they talked to me, I would explode, run into my room, slam the door shut, and lock myself in for a couple of hours. When I came out, my body language made it clear to them that I was sorry, but I would never verbalize those feelings. For example, I might do the dishes, vacuum the floor, and wash car to seek forgiveness. If my parents kept their peace with me under these circumstances—either using their body language or verbally accepting me, I would feel extremely touched. I would repent and be determined not to make the same mistakes again.

I respect my friends' opinion

During this stage of growth, I tend to seek my Friends' opinions. I try to learn life's philosophy from them. I value their points of view. I prefer their company and I want to identify with them. During this stage of life, I only like friends of the same sex. I am not interested in the opposite sex. I am enthused about extra curricular activities. Outside my house, my good behavior gets complimented. My peers welcome me.

In my house, I would act very polite toward guests- even act shy in front of strangers. When the guests leave, my true self resurfaces. My mother does not understand why I complain so much about my body - too skinny here and too fat there. I complain that the Creator is unfair to make me so ugly and I complain that my parents do not care about me nor love me. I think they are totally annoyed by me.

I daydream often

All of a sudden, I discover that some parts of my body are

different from before. Sometimes I stay in my room to examine my body, which the Creator has given me. I as a boy discover that my foreskin is not open. My friend does not urinate in the same manner as I do. That really irritates me. During this period of time, I start to have some sexual fantasy. I wonder when I will become the prince on the white horse and meet the love of my dreams. I wonder what kind of person I will become.

During this period, I also like to read jokes and comedies to amuse myself. I start to improve my abstract thinking. I have more and awkward and strong yet changeable, subjective opinions. I am often self-centered.

II. Mid adolescence- when I am fourteen to seventeen years old, I resent being controlled by adults.

I resent being controlled by adults

I start to discover that my parents are truly old-fashioned. Their way of thinking, their concepts, and their attitudes toward life are all out of date. I hate the way they keep harping at things. I am really turned off by them. How nice it would be if they just let me live my life- free to do anything. Whenever I have a conversation with them, they lecture me on their old-fashioned views. I am so annoyed by them that often we argue. Honestly, I never had any serious conflicts with them before until now. But I figure that the situation is already at it's worst so I let everything continue. I want to see how far they will allow me to rebel. I want to test their patience. Who told them to interfere with my freedom? If they continue disturbing me, I will run away one day so they will never find me.

My parents do not understand or love me. However, my friend next door understands and cares about me. He treats me as his buddy. Of course, I love to spend time with him. Whenever we are together, we are very happy. We enjoy listening to the same music, going to parties together, wearing strange clothes, and having unusual hairstyles. Look, we are different from the majority of people and are almost a different species. We talk on the phone constantly. His life is my life. I will do my best to solve his problems. Homework? We do them when we have time, but school is not important.

At different times we make even do risky things, which excites us. We go to parties where boys and girls embrace and dance. Parties are great! We smoke, drink, and chat. We even see people smoke pot. Although I haven't tried this, I'm excited about this experience.

I met a very charming girl who tells me that her parents are never home. She is lonely and her parents do not understand her. So, she finds comfort from her friends and marijuana. Her parents care very little about her. They seldom say, "I love you" to her. So she seeks love from her male friends and even has sex with them. She never finds the love she needs for her to feel complete. Sometimes I feel that I am in the same situation as she.

I feel empty inside

When I come home after a party, I often lay in bed contemplating about my life, especially the excitement and happiness from the party.

When those feelings disappear rapidly, I end up feeling lonely and empty. Then, I ponder many questions such as "who am I", "why was I born", or "what is the purpose of my being". I feel that not many people are smarter than I and that I am superior to others. I have good grades, being athletic, and popular. I try to be a good student at school and an obedient child to my parents. But, why do I still feel so lonely and empty? Life is like a big puzzle. No matter how I try to put it together, there is always one piece missing.

The inside and outside of me are at war

Who am I? I have yellow skin on the outside, but I am white inside. My friends tease me that I'm a "banana". My parents live with old Chinese Traditions while my school educates me with Anglo-Saxon culture. I am sandwiched in not knowing what to do. There is so much freedom at my friend's house, but at home I have a strict, stifling parents. I am not sure if the tradition, the faith, and the values that my parents taught me that are right for me. I do not feel comfortable refusing my parents guidance, yet when I accept my parents' values, I am very different from my friends. I think I need to rearrange my thinking, perhaps modeling my ideas after a very influential friend. I don't think I can find the best answer, but I just need to keep this fear inside of me for a while.

I am full of conflicts

Of course, at different times I still want my parents' suggestions and opinions. After all, they have lived longer and have had more experiences. When I think how old fashioned they are, I hesitate. The worst is whenever I gather enough courage to ask them for advice.

The answers that they give me are often things I do not want to hear. I have to admit that their answers are often very valuable; however, I am caught between a rock and a hard place. I teeter-totter between accepting and rejecting my parents' opinion and I am making them very confused. Deep down, I truly respect their opinions. I am just afraid to let them know about my emotional struggles and conflicts. When I grow up, I know that I will value their values and morals, as they are my models in life.

I have some friend who never had the opportunity to become friends with their parents. Many have problems with family communication. Some friends go out all of the time in search of a new friend. Some of them become addicted to alcohol or cigarettes. Some even try marijuana and other drugs. When their parents scold them more, they act worse. They do everything from smoking to drinking to using drugs. They use cigarettes, liquor, and drugs to numb themselves because they do not get any respect or love from home. Their own parents often look down upon them.

I am told from the expert that the truth is that if parents can accept their children as they are and are willing to listen to them, their children will not stray from the right path. According to some experts, experimentation with cigarettes, wine, and marijuana is the beginning that will often lead to harder drugs such as heroin, cocaine, and amphetamines.

I start to desire love

Being a boy, I realize, as I grow older that I am pleased when I see an attractive girl with a sweet smile. I am crazy about the way she walks, her big bright eyes, her long flowing hair, and her nice voice. When I see her, my heart starts pounding. I feel like I am on a cloud and think about her day and night. How wonderful it would be if I could only see her and spend time with her. I do not want other people to know my secret that I want to be her lover.

Yet, I think I'm in love. I don't know how to behave sometimes when I'm around her. I often ask my friends if I look sexy just because I want to win her heart, but I heard that girls are not as attracted to boy's appearances despite what my friends say. I discovered that I am attracted towards many girls' changes. My love for them lasts from weeks to months, only until another attractive girl appears.

III. Late Adolescence- When I am 17 to 21 years old, my relationship with my parents improves.

Improved relationship

As I grow older, I start to reflect on the bitterness from arguments with my parents by looking at those times from my parent's point of view. Our rapport improves because I understand their thinking, care, and love; thus, I feel closer to them than ever. Because of the improved relationship, I begin to show my love towards my parents, siblings, and relatives. I discover that I am a valuable member of my family when my parents provide me with greater freedom and responsibility.

I can accept my parents' opinion

At this age, I am more motivated to learn since I realize my future is determined by my academics. When my parents realize that I am working towards my career and goals, our communication improves. It's amazing because I am gradually able to accept my parent's value system. My parents, in turn, are willing to be open and honest with me. I am beginning to learn from their ideas, which I dismissed in the past, and I find that my ideas are rooted from theirs. I realize that I can accept their opinions. Now, my family provides me with a deal of comfort and affection.

I need guidance

There will be times when my parents and I still have different opinions regarding my future and college plans. They strongly feel that I should attend a college near home, but I feel that I need to go someplace far away to find myself and to begin my future. I don't want any conflicts with them. We discuss these matters and I am amazed at how flexible they are with me. In fact, they respect me. Maybe I might accept their opinions.

At this age, what I care most would be my parents and my future. Without guidance from my parents and family members, I would feel like a ship without a compass, not knowing right from wrong. Later on I have learned that often wrong concepts cause abnormal behavior and may prolong the adolescence's dependency on their parents. After graduating from high school, I decide to attend a university (or start a job) with my parent's consent. I also notice that my good friends and I are beginning to fend for us after graduating from high school. Even though they are my friends, we are all heading in different directions, sometimes weakening our friendship. I also am finding new friends from all walks of life. I can only keep my past good friends in my heart, but those friends may not feel the same way. I realize that the love from my family never changes. This naturally warms my soul. My family is the greatest treasure in my life.

I need to adjust myself to my new environment

From the first semester at college, I face many new challenges since life in college and high school are totally different. Studying with the nation's cream of the crop is stressful yet exciting. The professors impart so much knowledge and provide little time to master the material in addition to reading assignments and completing papers. I often feel out of breath. At the same time, I work with my classmates who become good friends as we work together, but sometimes these classmates discourage me from doing my best. This is why choosing which group to belong to be is a big challenge.

The lifestyles of some college students are very strange. Many study all night during the weekdays, but once the weekend comes, the whole group heads for parties. Males and females often view each other with mutual respect and become friends easily. I often find that there is no peer pressure like in high school. Therefore, I don't have to compromise any differences. I have plenty of room to do whatever I prefer.

I wish my parents understand me

I am very touched by my parents' love when I return home from college. But sure enough, my parents start asking about my personal life, especially whom I am dating. When I tell them about my dates and the parties, they react in horror and are speechless since they don't understand the lifestyle of a younger generation. They worry about me, which makes me very uncomfortable. I wish they could become my intimate friends and understand my feelings.

My heart goes out for my parents when I see how the "empty nest" syndrome impacted them. I understand their feelings and their desire to see me excel in life. They also worry about some bad habits in college. I appreciate their tender loving care towards me, but I am no longer a child. I try my best to be independent. I am very grateful for the years of love and care my parents have given to me. I understand them better and am able to accept their value system.

Summary of issues in Early, Middle, and Late Adolescence

Variation	Early Adolescence	Middle Adolescence	Late Adolescence
Age (yr)	10 - 13	14 -16	17 -20 and beyond
Sexual maturity rate	1 -2	3 -5	5
Sexual	Sexual interest exceeds, sexual activities	Sexual drive, experimentation, sexual orientation	Consolidation of sexual identity
Somatic	Rapid growth, awkward Height peaks, 2nd sex characteristics	Acne order, menarche; spermarche	Slow growth
Self-control	Self consciousness	Concern with attractiveness, increased introspection	Stable body image
Family	Bids for independence, Ambivalence	Struggle for acceptance of greater autonomy	Practical independenc
Peer	Same-sex group; Conformity; cliques	Dating; peer group less important	Intimacy; possibly commitment
'elation to society	Middle school adjustmen	Gauging skills; and opportunities	Career decisions

4

Spiritual Growth

Generally, family and school pay attention to the adolescent's physical and emotional growth as well as their academic and social skills. Parents and teachers all want adolescents to grow up in a friendly and happy environment. Even though adolescents joke around with their friends, excel at their academics, have many friends, they may also feel as if something is missing in life. This may be especially true when all is quiet at night. This feeling is normal because when God created man. He put a spirit inside humans. As a result, we naturally have the desire to find our roots. Mankind needs spiritual growth to find everlasting happiness.

A human being is made of three parts- spirit, soul, and body. After eight to ten years of physical growth, the body has matured, and the focus of growth turns inward. The soul includes reasoning, emotion, intelligence, happiness, and sadness. The soul provides a drive and dreams. In essence, our soul is what makes us human. We receive continual education and influence from our culture, parents, and friends to cultivate our personalities. In addition to the body and soul is the human spirit. The spirit is beyond the rational or the logical. Mankind has a desire to seek the spirit in order to answer fundamental questions including those about the self. Seeking answers about the spirit settles issues regarding life after death, good versus evil, and belief in a God. The spirit cannot be molded by philosophical doctrines, but by the journey through faith. This journey includes life experiences and our surroundings.

Knowledge of the Creator

Children, before the age of eight years can understand that there is a Creator in the universe. However, they may think God and humans are the same. Many children may also think that they know about God, but have a hard time rationalizing that God is omnipresent. Children derive their concept of God from their parents. For example, if parents are atheists, their child's concept of God will be very blurry. After eight years old, Christian children begin to understand that the Creator knows all, can do all, and can be everywhere. From nine and ten years old, they can understand that Easter has something to do with Jesus, but nothing to do with God. They feel that Jesus' resurrection is something thought up by man. In fact, the Resurrection is often a hard concept for children to understand. They often view God as an old man with a white beard wearing a long flowing robe. In their later years, they are more likely to understand that the Creator is a spirit.

After the age of ten, children's understanding of God is still centered on themselves. Gradually, they are able to separate God from mankind because they begin to understand the idea of spirit. Around the ages of eleven to thirteen, an important turning point in their faith may occur. They realize that God is not a human being and God is omnipresent- that He is with them every moment in their lives. He is the spirit in the universe. Typically after thirteen years old, they have a more concrete understanding of God. These adolescents know He is the master of all things. He controls all living things. Their lives are in God's hands. Their understanding of their faith grows more solid. After fourteen years old, they understand that the Bible is a book written by many authors based on actual experiences.

After the age of fourteen, adolescents can conceptualize that God reveals the Bible. This concept is of great importance. They begin to have a strong desire to pursue their faith. Gradually, their abstract concept matures. Their spiritual needs increase as they develop. They feel that mankind is very minute. As mere humans, our own effort often fails. The void of the soul cannot be satisfied only with education or material goods. In fact, statistics show that the age group between fourteen to eighteen years ranks as the highest period for accepting God.

The spirit of mankind is above all living things. The dissatisfaction of the spirit will cause unhappiness of the soul and body. Therefore, mankind has the tendency to search for God and to understand the meaning of life. One of the greatest philosophers of the middle ages, Saint Augustine, found the answer to this search. He said that the depth of the soul is a big void, which could not be satisfied with money, education, achievement, affection, or materials. It was not until the spirit of the Creator entered the depth of his soul that he received everlasting satisfaction. He then fully realized the true meaning of life. Saint Augustine's experience is also yours and mine. We are always searching for the unchangeable truth. We seek value in our lives in order to make it more meaningful and worthwhile.

Not uncommonly, people usually use looks, money, and talent as standards to measure against others. For example, many adolescents often suffer inferiority complexes because they feel that they cannot measure up to these standards. Consequently, they feel inadequate and may withdraw into themselves. They may become very lonely and susceptible to pain. The following is a journal from an adolescent:

I have always thought that nobody fully understood the hurt, pain, and loneliness of my soul. However, I discovered the truth. The master and creator of my soul have watched over me with endless love. Since my birth, He has cared for me and guided me. He knows the thirst of my soul. He understands my fears and failures. He wants me to return to Him because He is my root. He wants me to know that I belong to Him. He loves me and proved it by sending Jesus to this world to reveal Himself. He has let me know that even if I was the only one on earth, Jesus was still willing to die for me on the cross. He loves me and accepts me. How can I not accept myself?

When I know that people judge me by my looks, wealth, or talent, I feel very uncomfortable since these are man's standards, not God's. God tells me that everyone is valuable and He has chosen us. We are His children. Therefore, worldly standards cannot shake our positions. "What is highly valued among men is detestable in God's sight" (Luke 16:15). What mankind values are detested by God because this destroys our confidence and hinders us from obeying God's commands. Mankind uses these superficial value concepts to measure the value of our existence. Therefore, God detests these standards.

Later on, I find a secure and private place. I listen to all of my troubling problems and innermost thoughts. I ponder all of my worries. I examine my behavior, my patience, my pains, and my failures. I feel uneasy with all problems big or small. Without reservation, I write them all down and trust all to Jesus. I asked Him to bear the burden for me. This is my prayer.

Dear Lord Jesus:

Today I bring in front of you all of my problems and worries because you are the dearest of all my friends. You know all of my pain, weaknesses, strengths, failures, and frustrations because you have created me. I am writing this to list all of my problems and to show that I am totally in your hands. Forgive me. Cleanse me of all my imperfections. I am willing to open the door to my soul. Please enter my heart. Walk with me all of my life. Use me whatever way you please. As long as it is Your will, I will accept. Please mold me into someone you find favor with so I will no longer feel sad about my imperfections. Take my hand and guide me through my life. Amen.

When I prayed earnestly, my heart was full of tender love from God. He gave me peace and assurance since hearing my prayer. He changed me. He filled my life with love and peace. After I opened my heart and invited Jesus to come into my life to walk with me, knowing that He forgave my sins and all the imperfections, my life completely changed. I truly wish that the whole world would know. "Therefore, if anyone is in Christ, he is a new creation. The old has gone and the new has come!" (II Corinthians 5:17) If you and I have had the same experience, why not try this prayer. Make a list of all of your concerns. Trust God. I assure you that Jesus loves you. He has waited for you. Let Him guide you through your life.

I later learned one precious lesson. The Lord allows trouble and suffering to happen because He has a very special plan for us. He wants to use these difficulties as valuable experiences. He wants us to have the same spirit and optimism as His Son, Jesus Christ. He wants us to learn how to be more sensitive as well as more tolerant of others because "... in all things God works for the good of those who love him..."

After I learned how much God loves me by giving me His only Son to die for me, I have become very happy. Jesus is willing to travel my life's journey with me. If He loves us before we become His children, how much more will He love us after we become His? God not only loves us, He also gives us the Holy Spirit to walk, to live, and to share with us throughout life. He also prepares for us the love of our parents and siblings. They are there to guide, to understand, and to support us. We are so lucky! Through the Bible, God tells us that people before us suffered similar problems. But God is trustworthy. He will never let us suffer more than we can bear. When the time comes, He will show us a way so that we may bear the burden.

At different times, someone else has once experienced every problem. That is why the Bible records so many stories. These stories tell us that we are not alone in that experience. More importantly, the moral of the stories is that we can lead victorious lives if we trust God just as other people who have experienced similar struggles have.

QUESTIONS FOR PARENTS

1). As parents, how much do you know the physical growth of your adolescent? How do you react to your daughter's mood swings when she is menstruating? How do you react to your son's mood swings during his period of puberty?

2). During what period of adolescence is most rebellious against authority? During what period of emotional grows is the adolescent most easily influenced by peer pressure?

3). Spiritual growth affects physical and emotional growth of adolescence. What is your attitude toward the cultivation of your adolescent's spiritual growth? Do you encourage or prohibit spiritual pursuit? Do you show your unhappiness through your body language? Do you think that showing unhappiness increases the distance in your relationship?

4). How do you view adolescent dating? When you meet their dates, what is your attitude? What is your reaction? Are you relaxed or nervous? Do you care at all? Do you ask endless questions? Do you forbid them from dating?

5). What is your attitude about their usage of the telephone? Do you feel it is endless? Do you allow them a private telephone line? How would you deal with a high telephone bill?

6). Consider this: the adolescent's non-conforming actions, clothes, and speech turn us off.
How do you explain to your teen your position and views?

7). When your child returns home very late from a party after you waited up for him or her, what is your attitude? Do you welcome or do you scold your son or daughter?

8). Is the communication between you and your adolescent open? Are there some matters that you must discuss with them? Do you keep avoiding these matters? What do you do?

9). Do you plan your child's education, extra-curricular activities, and career? Do you have an opportunity to discuss these matters with them? If you cannot discuss with them freely, what would you do? Do they dare bring their problems to you?

10). How is your relationship with your adolescent? Do you feel comfortable enough to tell of your past failures and successes? Do you share your romantic history with them? Do they dare to tell you their secrets and ask for your opinion?

11). Do you have an opportunity to spend some time alone with your adolescent?
Can you confide in each other?

12). When you have done something wrong, do you have the courage to apologize and to ask for forgiveness from your teen? Or do you feel that since you are a parent, you do not need to apologize so you would not lose any respect.

QUESTIONS FOR ADOLECENTS

1). How do you perceive your parents? What kind of people do you think they are?

Are they very old fashioned? Are they very reserved? Are they very closed-minded?

Or are they open-minded? Are they fashionable and are receptive to new concepts?

2). What is your biggest obstacle when you talk to your parents? Can you express your deepest desire to them?

3). When you tell your parents your problem or trouble, what are their reactions? Are they usually surprised? Are they angered? Are they receptive? Are they very understanding? Are they sympathetic?

4). When you have problems, do you try to solve them by asking your parents first?

If you do, whom do you ask first- your mother or your father?

5). How are your relationships with your friends? Do they understand you and give you opinions? When their opinions and advice differ from your parents', whose opinion and advice do you take?

6). How do you treat your friends of the opposite sex? Do you tell your parents when you start dating or do you wait until you go steady? What is your view on premarital sex?

7). How do you cope with peer pressure? What is your attitude, "Everybody does it"?

What about when your conscience tells you not to do it? What do you do?

8). Have you wondered about your purpose in life? Are you happy with yourself?
How do you take care of any emptiness in your soul?

9). Do you dare to be different from your friends? Do you dare say "No" in front of your friends?

10). Have you ever considered that besides your parents, there is God, who loves you, cares about you, and is willing to travel life's journey with you?

11). Do you have plans for your future? Do you know how to achieve them? Do you have an opportunity to share and discuss these plans with your family?

12). Have you ever considered having a family? How and when do you accomplish this goal?

5

Inferiority Complex

During the growth years, I have discovered that my inferiority complex is my greatest enemy. I always felt that nobody liked me. I also felt that others were better than I in so many ways was. I'm a total failure and life is not worth living. I'm not smart or pretty. I have no special talent. Members of the opposite sex ignore me.

After talking to my best friend, I realize that other friends and classmates have similar worries. My boy friends think they are too short, too fat, and too skinny, have too many pimples or too many freckles. They even complain that they have too big or too small hands and feet. My girl friends complain that they are too tall, too fat, or too short. Also, they complain that they are just ugly. I often look in a mirror to pick out every defect that God created in me.

I dare say that there is not a single adolescent who is happy with the image in the mirror. The fact is that no one is a perfect. We should know that extreme dissatisfaction with one's appearance could cause shyness and abnormal sensitivity.

Parents should be very careful in what they say or do. Otherwise, they may unintentionally induce an inferiority complex in their children. When parents are tired from stress or a hard workday, they may be easily annoyed and irritated. It is at these times when they say things inadvertently. Little do they know that children will always remember this hurtful words - sometimes for the rest of their lives?

This is often one of the reasons some children feel that they are stupid while growing up. This is a reason why youths in junior and senior high schools suffer from inferiority complexes.

The second reason of having an inferiority complex is that adolescents often feel that they are not smart enough or are too stupid. This feeling germinates at an earlier age when they encountered difficulty reading or answering questions in class. This started to sprout during adolescence when experiencing adversity. If this persists, adolescent develops an inferiority complex. The inferiority complex will become a vicious cycle resulting from the lack of confidence in addition to losing motivation to studying to not studying.

The third cause of an inferiority complex is a financial one. Young people often feel that families who have beautiful clothes, elegant homes, and parents in respected professions are superior. Young people will look at their lives and their possessions as a means to justify their place in society. Wearing outdated clothes or having humble origins, some adolescents will start to have an inferiority complex. If an adolescent discovers that they lack all three, they will be more likely to feel inferior.

Some experts reveal that eighty percent (80%) of American adolescents do not like their appearance. They are often exasperated by their looks. They often wish to wake up one morning to see their defects disappear. However, when I look around me, I discover that many people suffer differing degrees of inferiority. They use different means to show their fears and worries. Some become shy and introverted. Some become temperamental. Others may act tough or silly. Others may blush easily. Others appear arrogant. It is important to let adolescents know they are not alone. An inferiority complex is a very common phenomenon. Other people feel the same way. Everybody, at any age, is afraid of encountering embarrassing situations and nobody wants to be the laughing stock. After all, we are all in the same leaky boat. Everyone tries to stop the holes in the boat. Knowing this helps increase confidence immediately.

At times, problems or troubling thoughts will eat at my soul, making me feel discouraged. Fortunately, I have found in church a very trustworthy youth counselor who understands adolescents well. I discus with him my problems and honestly tell him my feelings. I ask for his advice. I learn that other people have experienced the problems I face today, as well. However, they can all be overcome. I learned a great deal from other people's experiences; thus, I solve many of my own problems. The church counselor encourages me to spell out all my innermost worries in order to shed my burden. I follow his advice and write down all needs and worries on a sheet of paper. When I tell God my worries and problems, I ask for His wisdom and guidance. My heart is filled with his gentle love and assurance. I am now able to concentrate my energies to make up for my weakness. In other words, I focus on my talents to compensate for my perceived flaws. For example, if appearances do not determine one's value, why cares so much about looks? It is better to use my energy and effort on things I like to do. If I can excel in academics, music, or sports, I can build up my self-confidence by concentrating on these areas. My peers for who I am and not just by how I look can accept me. When I excel in one thing, I will not feel quite as bad when I do not win a popularity contest. My unique talents gradually make me like myself better. I find out that when I like myself, other people begin to like me as well.

Only true friends can help us build our self-confidence. True friends are not necessarily the one with the good looks or extraordinary talents. True friends are the ones who like me for me. When I am well liked, it is easier for me to accept myself. However, there is another truth. It is easier to make good friends if I become someone else's good friend first. When someone is suffering the same problem as I do, I will try to be there and earn his or her trust. I will make him feel that I respect and accept them. I will not tease or jokingly express my opinions. If I treat others well, they will remember me and seek opportunity to reciprocate. I was very surprised to find out that if I give my helping hand, I will gain self-confidence as well as friendship. A Christian friend told me he is going to help those people who feel inferior because they are also God's children. Jesus teaches us: "Whatever you did for one of the least of these brothers of mine, you did for me" (Matthew 25:40).

6

Peer Pressure

Since birth, humans depend on the continual nurture and support from parents and family. Friends also play an important role in our lives. No matter what stage we are in our lives, friends make our lives more enjoyable and meaningful. Nobody can live alone on a deserted island. We need friends to add color to our lives, making our lives more interesting.

Adolescents are influenced by environment.

There are three elements that affect the growth of adolescence: 1) parents and family members, 2) friends, and 3) environment. The environmental element is one that often causes adolescents to take great risks- sometimes against their better judgment.

When adolescents interact socially, peer pressure is often very difficult to resist. This is especially true in a new environment when an adolescent wants to be accepted by new friends. In order to feel accepted, an adolescent may behave like their peers. For example, they begin to wear similar types of clothing, have the same style of haircut, use similar language, and act in a manner like their friends. They do this subconsciously believing that the quickest and safest way to be accepted is through conformity.

Sometimes, there is an unwritten and unspoken rule among them. That is, "if you want to be our friend, you must do as we do." In order to avoid being embarrassed or despised, a teen will take risks to win what is believed to be a trusting friendship. Thus, the adolescent unknowingly follows the crowd in order to achieve acceptance.

The following is a confession of an adolescent:

"Before I was fully accepted by my friends, I was willing to pay a dear price to get it. I truly disliked being alone. I felt aimless without friends. I could not describe the thrill and happiness when I finally was accepted and respected by my friends. That kind of feeling was far more important than anything my family could have given me. I always felt that my parents did not understand me nor did they care about me. Sometimes, I felt that they did not totally love me, either. After I turned thirteen, I felt like I was no longer a child. I should be on my own. I would soon grow up. I should solve my own problems. My friends gave me the kind of freedom that my parents rarely allowed.

"Later I discovered that only fifteen percent (15%) of adolescents obediently accept their parents' guidance during this period. Eighty-five percent (85%) of adolescents do not believe what they are told by or informed about by their parents until they have tested out things themselves. They want to set their own guidelines of making friends and dealing with life matters.

"Between the ages of eleven and fourteen I asked my parents several times if I had an abnormal body. It seemed that I had quite a bit of fat all over me. My body had expanded like a balloon- into one that was quite different from the past. My parents were too uncomfortable to answer me clearly. When I asked my friends, they told me that I was one hundred percent(100%) normal. Not only that, some of them even showed me their bodies for comparison. I was finally at ease.

"I had some good friends who were serious about their studies. They got good grades and excelled in sports. Some even had good manners. So I invited them to my house to play and to study. I was so grateful that my parents welcomed them with open arms. My friends would ask questions in order to understand my parents or were at the least polite to them. Frequently, my parents became friends with them. Therefore, my friends liked to come to my house. However, my mother insisted on one rule. We should not close the door when we would study or play in the same room. At first I did not understand her reasoning. I knew later that her intention was to be aware of what we were doing. She was training us to be open and honest.

"Good friends have led me down the right path and given solid values. At times, I had some friends who used bad language. Unintentionally, I copied their bad expressions. I just could not help myself. On one hand, I knew my parents would not be happy if they heard us using swear words or being crude. I knew that my parents would not want me to hang out with these friends. On the other hand, I wanted to keep these friends. Fortunately, my parents noticed the situation. They used clever methods to rescue me before I embarrassed myself. They gently persuaded me to set a higher goal in life by finding and making more respectful friends.

"Often I wondered why my parents used such traditional Chinese values to guide me. What I learned from school generally was the American culture. I often felt as if I was caught between these two cultural values. I went through a period of self-examination. I would have so many questions. Who am I? Why do I feel so much tension and disharmony? I felt like I was All-American on the inside- as if I were "white". However, my physical features definitely told the world that I am Asian. I was definitely aware that my skin color was "yellow. Some friends and I would even joke and say that we were bananas.

"My physical attributes are not the only thing that made my community realize my Asian heritage. Some of the odd things I had to endure to please my parents also told everyone that I was not Caucasian. For instance: one day my mother made me wear clothes that were sent from overseas by my grandmother. Everybody at school wore large loose clothes with cool brands from hip stores. Even though the clothing my grandmother sent me what was in fashion overseas, my classmates all laughed at me. They said that I looked ridiculous- like I was "fresh off the boat." I was so embarrassed! I could have died of embarrassment. As soon as the school bell rang, I disappeared. I swore that I would never wear strange clothes to school any more even if my mother tried to force me.

"It was not just wearing those clothes from overseas that caused my turmoil. I also felt the pressure from my parents to succeed academically at school. Some of my classmates studied very hard. They made good grades and could go to well-known colleges or universities, like Harvard or Stanford. I tried to do the same. Once, however, I failed my test. My teacher openly discussed the matter in front of the classroom. I was so embarrassed! Worse yet, my parents were furious. I made up my mind to study harder but I still had the pain of failure. Fortunately my friends from the church group understood me. They encouraged me and cared about me. Together we prayed for God's wisdom and that He would give me confidence to keep trying my best. I sympathized with those classmates who could not catch up with their studies. I knew how they must have felt. Who would care about them?

"Though my studies were an area that caused me a great deal of stress, I also had other concerns. I noticed around the time I was fourteen to seventeen, some of my friends started to show an interest in the members of the opposite sex. In fact, some started dating. They would vividly describe the exciting stories of their dates and maybe even their sexual experiences. I longed to follow in their footsteps. But I faced it with some dilemma. My good buddies took me to parties. They danced, drank, and smoked cigarettes. Some smoked pot and other drugs. Some engaged in sexual activities. They embraced girls and danced, seemingly having a great time. They challenged me to follow suit. I was afraid to do so because I figured if my parents found out what I was doing, they would kill me.

"My friends' challenges made me nervous and confused. They teased me by saying that I was still holding on to my mother's apron string. They claimed that I was a coward and that I would never grow up. They wanted me to prove to them that I could do what they did. During this critical moment, I wished that my parents were by my side to give me advice but at the same time I did not think I could talk to them about this. Someone once told me: Parental guidance at an adolescent's crossroads is so very important. I prayed to God to ask for His help and discernment to be victorious in my struggle.

"I asked the youth counselor at my church about his opinions on dating. He told me that after an extended study on divorced couples, he had reached a critical conclusion. He said that whatever pattern set during the courtship would determine the success of a marriage. It is hard for youths as well as adults to comprehend how much influence the behavior displayed while dating plays in marriage."

The following guidelines from experts determine if an adolescent is mature enough to date:
1). When one understands the benefits and dangers of dating.
2). When one understands what God reveals in the Bible about dating.
3). When one is strong enough to not compromise his or her standards and values, even if it means losing opportunities to date.

The fact of the matter is that some people have sexual contact while they are dating. Sometimes, this happens before they begin to develop the mental or spiritual communication. This is not love, but infatuation. They do not truly understand each other. They do not know if they have compatible personalities. When the romantic feelings fade, they have nothing to talk about or anything in common. They are like two total strangers. When that happens, they feel hurt spiritually and emotionally.

God wants people to proceed with spiritual communication, to share with each other the wonders of life, and to gradually build up intellectual, rational, and emotional unity. Couples mutually sharing their likes and dislikes of daily living and work. Using God's faithfulness helps keep your chastity. Motivate and encourage each other to plan for the future. It is best to consummate physical intimacy on the wedding night.

In my adolescence, I have learned a very important fact. I know why adolescents suffer so much social pressure. We fear rejection by our companions. As a result, we try very hard to imitate our friends' actions. Why can we not think or act independently? It is because we do not fully accept and like ourselves. We lack self-confidence. We want to avoid the embarrassment of thinking that people are laughing at us. We do not want to be different from others. We do not want to express differing opinions in the event we get scolded and teased. An inferiority complex plays tricks on our psyche. We think if we identify with others, nobody will tease or taunt us.

Lacking the courage to "dare to be different" is a by-product of an inferiority complex. However, conformity can be very dangerous when you are with your friends. Think about this scenario: You and three friends are driving around in a car. A short time later one of your friends takes out four red pills from his pocket. He pops one into his mouth and gives a pill each to the other two friends who also swallow the red pills. Only you are left.

You know it is wrong to swallow the red pill because it is a drug. You waver because your conscience tells you not to do it. In the mean time, your friends are teasing you, saying: "you are a coward," "you are a mama's boy," "you will never grow up." In addition, they tempt you by saying that you will like it. If you agree to it and swallow that red pill, they will regard you as their good friend. They will give you the pill again the next time you are together. They will convince you by saying that you have already taken it before. Why are you refusing it now? Repeated occurrences will gradually turn you into a drug addict. This is the reason why so many youths become addicted to alcohol, cigarettes, and dangerous drugs.

If you dare to be different under this type of pressure, it is likely that they will not invite you along in the future. It takes self-confidence, but those who have it can let them know that "if you want to pop pills, go ahead. I respect your choice, but I think it is wrong so I won't take it. " By saying so you show your friends that you have the courage to state your opposing view. Moreover, they may not think so at the time but secretly they respect you for your courage and willpower. People who possess this type of confidence and willpower eventually become brave and able leaders. Those who stand up against environmental influences are the ones who help others fight peer pressure.

The greatest challenge during the growth of adolescence is self-control. When we are young, our parents set behavior limits for us. Sometimes, we will disregard our parental standards to see what would happen if we did not abide within those limits. We will also compare our parents' standards with other parents' standards. As I grow up I find that what I believed to be unacceptable values of my parents have now become my own guidelines. When I was twenty years old I realized that I play an important role in the society as well as in my family. I gradually understood the value of my parents' guidance. At the time, I did not realize that my parents are an excellent source of advice. Now, I believe one day when I have my own children, I will value my parents' loving discipline more than ever before. I will tell my experiences to my children. I will use my experiences as references and tools to help guide my own children.

7

The Formation of Self-Image

I. Definitions of Self-Image, Self-Identity, and Self-Esteem

People often use self-image, self-identity, and self-esteem synonymously. Each actually has it's own meaning.

Self-Image

Self-image is what adolescents feel about them. In other words, it is how adolescents view themselves.

In general, American youths are stereotypically blonde, blue-eyed, and fair complexion. If children aren't born with these characteristics, sometimes they may feel they are not good enough. Consequently, they will spend a great deal of time identifying with a role model. They will

Growth of Adolescence
❖

emulate that person in every way possible. Sometimes they will realize that they are not very successful in their imitation. They may try hard, but just can not cut it. They often feel worthless and have low self-image. Having a low self-image can turn teens bitter, sarcastic, and resentful. It will cause adolescents to loose their self-confidence.

Twenty percent (20%) of adolescents have a severe case of low self-image. They overly underestimate themselves. Some may commit suicide. Twenty percent (20%) have a healthy self-image. Another twenty percent (20%) do not like themselves often turning to self-pity (depression). The remaining forty percent (40%) are somewhere among the three categories.

Self-Identity

Self-identity involves in answering, "where do I fit in the grand scheme of things". In other words, finding and affirming a role in the society would be seeking self-identity. Adolescents want to know where they belong.

Self-Esteem

Self-esteem is built up by having a positive self-image and a clear self-identity. It means that one views himself or herself as a valuable human being who plays an important role in the scheme of life. If one does not have a good self-image, it will be difficult to achieve a clear self-image or a healthy self-esteem.

68

II. The Formation of Self-Image

Self-image is formed through a long period of time

Adolescents will not wake up one morning and confidently say, "I have a good self-image" or "I love myself". The environment gradually shapes self-image. During my adolescent years, I felt everyone was watching my every move. There was always an imaginary audience who listened to my every word and noticed what I wore or did. I thought that everybody had the same opinions as me. I thought that if I disliked myself, others disliked me too. Many experts call this ego-centralism. Either right or wrong, this pattern of thinking follows me likes a shadow becoming a distinct quality of my self-image. For example, a girl might spend one hour fixing her hair until perfection before she meets anybody.

I just cannot imitate that person

For a period of time, I was afraid of revealing my true personality. I assumed that if other people found out my true self, they would not like me any longer. So, I would adopt other people's lifestyle and habits. I would copy some popular musicians, movie stars, and athletes. After a short period of time, I realize that I couldn't mimic them. I'm simply me. Suddenly, I realized that my extreme limitation and feel depressed about who I really am. Hence, self-image may suffer a big blow.

III. How to Nurture a Healthy Self-Image

All of my life, I have tried to do my best hoping to be accepted and liked. Nevertheless, the typical adolescent receives approximately five thousand negative criticisms annually from parents, family, teachers, friends, and the media. Progressively, this negative criticism lowers self-image. Being positive and reinforcing the good will build self-image. Here are several guidelines.

I will accept myself

There is a difference between "self-improvement" and "self-acceptance". "Self-improvement" refers to changing the outside appearance to find self-image. "Self-acceptance" is simply accepting that some things could never change, such as bone structure, hair color, and complexion. I used to nit-pick every part of my body. I got miserable by doing so. Since I had decided to accept my true self, I felt better and peaceful.

I am God's unique creation

There is no other human being exactly like me. God has a specific purpose and plan for me since God knows my strengths, weaknesses, innate beauty, and potential. I am grateful for His many blessings. God accepts me for whom I am and comforts me in time of need. When I reflect on what God has done in my life, my self-image grows.

I will not compare

In the past, I often used to compare myself with others. I was often heartbroken as a result. Many sages advised never to do this. How right they were! At last, I have come to realize that no matter how talented a person is, still no one is perfect. Everyone has unique talents in different fields.

I will be prudent in what I say.

Not only that I have to be careful with others' negative and cruel criticism, I also have to be careful not to be too critical with myself. There are already plenty of people who look at me with tinted glasses. Why should I be a hard critic of myself? Now I know when I positively motivate other, and myself, not only do I feel assured of my position, but also my self-image is elevated. Consequently, I am able to help others grow as well.

IV. The development of identity formation

Two elements affect the birth of identity formation (personality, or characteristics.) One element is emotional, the other, social. The exterior element continuously molds our personalities. According to Erik Erickson, the development of a personality can be categorized into eight stages. An adolescent's identity formation is the product of the first five stages. A person's identity formation is people and environment and his/her reaction to them affect each stage. Since birth, a human being is affected by his /her surrounding moral-standards. If the moral-standards are extreme, he/she will acquire an extreme personality.

First state: Babyhood (before the age of one)—development of trust or mistrust

If parents or a baby-sitter trusts the baby, it will develop a trustworthy personality. The trusting experience will ultimately lead to an optimistic personality. On the contrary, if parents or the baby-sitter continually mistrusts a baby, it will develop an "I am not be trusted" personality.

Second stage: Toddler age (between the age of two and three)— development of autonomy or shame/doubt

Toddlers at this stage have a tendency to test the world by acts of insubordination. If parents' counteraction is firm and principled, the toddler will attain a cheerful and self-controlled personality. Otherwise, the toddler will attain a mistrusting personality.

Third stage: Playful age (between the ages of four and five)— development of initiative or guilt

Children have contacts with friends in the neighborhood and school. If they are in a group of children with high moral principles, they will obtain a decisive, keen foresight, and goal-oriented personality. Otherwise, they will have a despondent, passive, lazy, and dependent personality.

Fourth stage: Learning age (between the ages of six and eleven)— development of industry or inferiority

During this period of time, children who study hard have great desire to learn and improve themselves. If they receive positive reassurance, they will develop a spirited personality filled with self-confidence. Otherwise, they will develop an inferior personality, lacking confidence to accomplish any objectives. America is a country with many cultures; Chinese children usually do not comprehend the identity differences. At home they are Chinese, outside the house they are Americans.

Stage five: Adolescence (between the age of twelve and twenty-one)—development of sense of identity or clarification of roles

Between the ages of eleven and fourteen, adolescents pay a great dealt of attention to their bodies. They often ask themselves, "Who am I?" "Why is my body like this?" What kind of person will I become?" "Why am so fat? Between the ages of fourteen and seventeen, an adolescent's focus is on their feelings and members of the opposite sex. "Why am I still controlled by others? I do not want to be controlled. I have grown up!" They like members of opposite sex. However, their adored choices keep changing. Because of the rebellious tendency, adolescents will reevaluate their relationships with parents and friends. They want to pursue some kind of religion. Between the ages of seventeen and twenty-one, they are more certain of their identities. "What direction should I progress?" "What role should I play in my house?" They gradually have clearer concept of the above two questions. They have more correct outlook on marriage. Healthy growth during this stage will make an adolescent faithful, honest, and loyal. Otherwise, he/she will become confused of his/her identity, feeling flustered and confused of the roles they play.

During this stage, Chinese adolescents born and grown in the

United States can discern racial differences. They are able to identify their care and embrace their own tradition. However, when they collate the defect in the family with the merit of American families, they will feel that white culture is superior, thus, inducing some inferiority complex. Born of yellow race, they admire the white culture. This type of discord lasts for a few years. During college years, they will discover that their race is not inferior to any. Then, the self-confidence will be restored.

Most of the above-mentioned identity crisis takes place during adolescence because it is a time when adolescents want to get away from family control and try to establish their own values and independence. In that effort, adolescents may experience some anxiety, frustration, insomnia, or appetite loss. They may also lose interests in friends, school, or other activities. Luckily, it will only last a very short period of time. Normality will soon be restored.

V. Parental influence on the adolescent's self-esteem

Self-esteem starts at home. Parents are pivotal to adolescent's self-esteem. Therefore, it is vital to create a healthy condition for them because one does not attain self-esteem alone. Self-esteem is the culmination of family influence. Parents hold the key to nurture or destroy a child's self-esteem. The following are some suggestions:

1. Parents' constant affirmation, support, and love will establish adolescent self-esteem, particularly, when parents approve of their appearance and study habits. Generally, adolescents with high self-

esteem come from a family of strong parental acceptance, care and understanding. It can be summed up in one sentence, "Love nurtures self-esteem."

When parents' love is dubious, it will be difficult for adolescents to ascertain what a proper action is. Wishy-washy attitudes from parents will stunt adolescent's self-esteem.

2. Parents should not have unrealistic expectations of their offspring. In general, adolescents are already idealistic about their future. If parents' expectation surpasses adolescent's ability, they will sink into despair once they fail. Failure is not always harmful. But to fail to meet parents' expectation beyond his/her ability is surely detrimental to an adolescent self-esteem!

3. The style of parental discipline plays an important role in establishing self-esteem. A positive style of discipline means that parents demand adolescents to respect and keep the mutually agreed upon contracts. When parents have set clear rules and enforce them without compromises, they become good models of self-esteem.

4. Parents' self-esteem parallels adolescents' self-esteem. Adolescents learn more from their parents' actions than their words. No matter what a family's social status is, parents' high self-esteem will be a living model for their adolescents to form high self-esteem.

8

Meeting Friends, Dating and Marriage

I. Meeting friends:

The love relationship between a man and a woman is said to be a marvelous chemical reaction. It is described by poets with dazzling depiction, and has inspired numerous great composers to fill their musical work with splendor. Countless men and women would give everything for the sake of love, but few talk about the reality after marriage. This leads to an illusion that the meaning of love is to live a happily ever after.

Can a pure friendship exist between men and women? We may say that it is possible, but the relationship between men and women is very intricate. It is often mixed with the attraction to the opposite sex. The attraction is difficult to overcome if one is caught off guard while being irrational, or weak-willed, which usually leads to sexual impulses.

Some people believe in love at first sight. The man and the woman fall in love after first meeting, and immediately become inseparable, spending time together day in and day out. Rarely does this kind of instant love last. One could very well be in love with only the outer shell of this stranger, such as those enchanting eyes, the voice that melts hearts, and every part of this person seem to attract you like a magnet. Often, one is led to believe that love of his life. In reality, he does not really know who she is, does not know her interaction with others... etc. He has only gotten to know the outer shell. That is not true love at all. The past experiences of many have shown us that after two people get to know each other for some time, they will realize that an attractive outer appearance does not always speak for one's inner beauty. Therefore, the realization may lead to break up. This so-called "love" is only infatuation. These emotions are fleeting.

II. Dating:

Therefore, it is advisable to avoid the one-to-one dating scene until one's Emotional Quotient (EQ) reaches full maturity. When a man and a woman who are attracted to each other spend time together alone, they can easily be caught in the grip of passion. If one must date, it is best to go in a group with two or three other friends. A healthy relationship between the opposite genders can gradually develop through setting.

Most girls enjoy compliments from others and more readily to believe the promises made by guys. If he wants to pursue you, he vows to love you forever. Even though the seas run dry and the rocks crumble, he promises that his love for you will never change. But when he finally has your heart, you may discover the truth to the saying "never say never".

To the Girls:

Some guys can vow to love you at all cost, no matter what it takes. But this vow in reality is accompanied by conditions. Maybe you can bring him happiness, love, care, security, and satisfaction. But eventually, when something you do annoys him, or a conflict of interest arises, he may turn his back on you, or even become violent toward you, and abandon you.

When a guy meets a girl who is sexy, he may desire to get close with her physically, because he is sexually aroused. This desire is mostly impulsive rather than love-filled. When a mature man seeks a wife, he looks for someone with inner beauty, high standards of morality, and self-control. If a girl is too 'easy' by becoming intimate with a guy sexually involved, most likely he won't be too impressed with that girl. On the contrary, the guy will loose his respect and trust for the girl. He may think of her as flirtatious, "too easy" and even suspect her fidelity. In many boy-girl relationships (BGR), the ultimate desire of the guy is sex, but for the girl it is usually intimacy, not necessarily sex.

In general, the guy pursues the girl before the relationship becomes sexual.

But once a sexual relationship is developed, it changes to a girl-pursing-the guy type of relationship. If your boyfriend demands sex, what should you·do? Some girls may give in because they are afraid of losing their boyfriends. In reality, giving in can ruin the relationship. You can try responding by saying, "If you respect me, let us wait until we are married". If he leaves you because of this, it is your gain. A person who does not respect you does not desire your love. He is a selfish, irresponsible man. But if you give in to please him and allow him to push you to do things you are not ready for once, there will be a second, third and fourth... time in the future.

If an adolescent has already had sexual experiences, make it clear that it is never too late to make a commitment to reserve sex for marriage. This important concept is called "secondary virginity" and should be strongly encouraged among adolescents who have been sexually active. Some churches and parachurch organizations have formal programs organized specifically to promote the decision to remain sexually abstinent until marriage.

In societies, most men look down upon their wives having sexual experiences in their previous relationships. They don't want a 'left-over.' But many guys are eager to have a sexual-relationship with their girlfriends. First of all is to satisfy their pride. Secondly, they think that their girlfriends will stay with them once they are sexually involved. If your husband finds out that you are not a virgin, and is terribly bothered by that, would you have acted differently?

Therefore, true love is the kind of love that thinks about others. At times, it might even mean letting the other person go instead of thinking, "If I can not have her, then no one can". If you must date, do not tempt his self-control, do not wear outfits that are too revealing, say or do things that are seductive, or spend nights together...etc. Always remember that God is going with you on the date. He knows our every move. Because our bodies are the temples of God, do not defile them. You can cheat other people, but you can't cheat God Himself. You can begin to pray for your future spouse. Pray that God prepare you and your future spouse for one another and for the opportunity in the future. Dedicate yourself to follow the teachings of the Bible. Ask God to give you strength and courage to keep yourselves pure so that you may give the very best to each other.

In general, the intense passions between teen-age couples begin to cool down after two to three years. The beauty they once saw in each other begins to fade and no longer sparks the attraction for one another. After they get to know each other and face the cruel realization that they are not compatible, the couple often breaks up the realization. The scars of pain from the break-up will stay with them forever. Therefore, do not get married before the age of twenty, because statistics show that fifty percent (50%) of the married couples end up in a divorce after approximately seven years, and what is left are endless tears and heartache.

III. Marriage:

One day you will get married. Each individual holds a different set of criteria for choosing a life-long partner. Some look for beauty, wealth, intelligence, capability or specific ethnic background. I would like to recommend using the Biblical story of how Abraham sought a wife for his son Isaac as an example. At that time, Abraham and his whole family were living in Cannon, but they had a different faith and belief. Abraham sent a servant to his homeland, to his own tribe to seek for a godly woman. Through prayers and God's miraculous leading, he found Rebecca for Isaac. The story tells us that Rebecca was a beautiful and capable woman who feared the Lord and obeyed the arrangement of her parents in terms of whom to marry. Having a common faith was what Abraham saw as most important, because it shapes one's value system.

As soon as the issue of match making or referral by parents is mentioned, the youth usually will get very upset because it is against the current thought of the young generation. Actually, you are still struck and limited, regardless how much do you know and how many friends do you have. You are still growing, getting mature and lacking experiences. Sometimes owning to our immature one-sided viewpoints and value systems, we tend to make decision blindly. Your parents have more experiences and more mature thoughts. They have more experience than you do and they try to provide the best for you. Parents will never give you the worst. It won't be harmful, if you consider listening to what they offer and take a risk of meeting the friends they try to introduce to you. You can refuse them but try not to fight against your parents who love you dearly. You can discuss and share with them your opinions and they are more than willing to share with you about their experiences and their views.

Please remember that a marriage will not last long without the blessing from your parents and family members. You will be very lonely and fill with grief without your parental support during the hardships of your marriage. Abraham emphasized the essence of the belief, which will last forever. He certainly could choose the best girl among the gentiles for his son Isaac. However, the worldly conditions will change but the unique trust in God is everlasting and the religious value system is the foundation of the family. A family bestowed by

God may face difficulty and crisis. But through God's guidance, the outcome is entirely different from those without faith in God.

Many Christians married non-Christians in the past. They faced endless problems and headache dealing with many issues. For instances, offerings, attending Sunday worship, children's Christian schooling, and rearing the children in Christian atmosphere become the center of constant arguments. It is much easier to help the non-Christian spouse to convert before marriage. Once you get married, it is very difficult to help the husband/wife to the Lord. Premarital counseling is very important and essential for each other to understand the differences.

How about the inter-racial marriage? We will find the answer from the study of Jesus' pedigree. Apparently, there were a few foreign girls married to a Jewish family and they became the ancestors of Jesus Christ. These few women feared and worshiped God, the prerequisites of successful inter-racial marriage. The Bible does not prohibit the inter-racial marriage but it emphasizes the importance of the same beliefs, which will lay the foundation of the happy family.

Which marriage is superior between the western and eastern styles? Everybody has his own opinion. Dr. Hu Su-Tze, famous scholar of recent Chinese history expressed his own experience and opinion. The eastern marriage very often is match making or referred by family or extended family. The love sparks after the marriage which is initiated from mutual respect and understanding. This passion is just like the ignition of the boiling tea after the marriage and it will gradually burn to the boiling point as long as life goes on. The couple will know and love each other more and more from time being. Their love gets sweeter and sweeter just as enjoying the sugar cane. In western marriages, the couple gets together after they know each other so well before marriage. They marry at the maximum burning point. Some say there is nothing attractive any more after the marriage. On the other hand, the boiling water will gradually cooling down. The couple can end up in divorce so easily. The above different thoughts are quite interesting. You may consult your parents about their viewpoint as your reference.

IV. Some suggestions for marriage:

To the Parents:

Early adolescence is a good time to begin discussing with your child the characteristics and traits to seek in a future wife or husband. Some experts suggest that adolescents begin praying for wisdom in selecting their future spouse from the age of 12 years old. Marriage is established by God and is blessed by Him. The happy marriage will bring great joy and hope to the family. It is suggested that parents toward the end of high school, give your adolescent some books that explore the process of selecting partner and building a strong marriage. Two excellent books are Dr. James Dodson's "Love for a Lifetime" and "Finding the Love of Your Life", by psychologist Dr. Neil Warren.

The most important thing for the parents is to develop a healthy concept of marriage for your children by allowing them to see you love, cherish, and respect your partner. If you have children, allow them to spend time with other families to in which a nurturing, respectful marital relationship is modeled.

To the adolescents:

If you are not able to get long well with your parents, family members or roommates, you may have the same difficult adjusting to your future married life. The way you respond to your parental authority is the same way you will likely respond to your spouse. The daughter's attitude toward her father will probably be the same toward her husband. Similarly, the way the boy treats his mother is likely how he will treat his wife.

Many experts indicate that premarital sex may lead you to marry the wrong person and rob you of a satisfying lifelong marriage. Bear that in mind, this advice may not be well taken, however, if you were the parent, how would you like your children to behave. Children of divorced parents may be tempted to cohabit prior to marriage in hope of avoiding their parents' mistakes. But statistics indicate that cohabiters have an even greater chance of divorce.

Premarital counseling is very important. Through counseling, we are able to understand mutual differences, strengths, and weaknesses. Therefore, we are able to prepare ourselves. Counseling is not a waste of money but one step to build your happy marriage. There are no identical individuals in the world, only two imperfect people who will face difficulties and conflicts.

The following are the recommendations for Adolescents from the experts:

1. Don't get married too young. Wait to get married until you know yourself well, and until you know well the kind of person with

whom you can be happy.

2. Don't get married too quickly. Longer courtship will produce consistently healthy marriage.

3. Don't be too eager to get married, and don't let anyone else who is overly eager push you into marriage. Before marriage, be sure that your mind is clear and settled.

4. Don't try to please someone else with your choice. You are the one who will benefit or suffer from your marriage for a lifetime.

5. Don't marry someone until you know him or her in a lot of different ways. If your experience is broad, you may make a better prediction about the marriage.

6. Don't marry with unrealistic expectations. Marriage is not a panacea; it requires an incredible amount of hard work. Don't expect unrealistic goals from your marriage.

7. Don't marry anyone who has a personality or behavioral problem that you are not willing to live with forever. These problems do not vanish; in fact, they often get worse. If the problem can't be cured, make sure it is resolved before your commitment. Learn how to solve differences before marriage.

8. If your parents, relatives, and close friends support your contemplated marriage, celebrate with them, because they have a better view. If they do not support you, please listen carefully to them before you make your final decision. Marriage without the blessing and support from them is a bitter dead end you will regret.

9

Communication Skills with Adolescents

Anger, irritation, and communication

Parents in general have difficulty communicating with adolescents. It is because often times just saying one wrong word can trigger anger from adolescents. The truth is: it is not the wrong word that triggers the outburst. What was said and the tone used by the parents is the cause. Parents often get headaches trying to communicate with their adolescents afterwards since communication is highly unlikely. On the other hand, adolescents feel that they are not respected or understood. Therefore, the only method to show their dissatisfaction is through hostile emotions and outbursts.

The Reasons Adolescents Get Angry

1. Being hurt and disappointed can cause adolescents to get angry

because they lack the power to change a situation or solve a problem. When an adolescent loses his/her parent's support or is misunderstood by parents, he/she gets mad easily.

2. Parents may reproach adolescents because they do not know peers had misunderstood their child. When adolescents are unable to defend their innocence, they will become angry and frustrated.

3. When they feel totally inept to change their hurtful environment, adolescents will complain and get mad at family members, either to seek revenge or to let out steam.

4. Adolescents will feel angry when parents do not unconditionally accept them or fully understand them. Adolescents crave parental care and acceptance. If parents cannot satisfy their craving, adolescents will keep the disappointment inside, gradually becoming irritable.

Adolescents' Methods of Showing Irritation

1. Negative Resistance Method

It is the most commonly used method showing discontentment by using negative resistance to challenge authority. Adolescents will resist authority negatively if they feel impatient with their parents, teachers, or older siblings. At the end adolescents themselves are the ones who suffer the consequences. For example: an adolescent might use poor grades to show his/her anger, the indulgence of pre-marital sex may be to challenge family morals, or the use of alcohol and drugs to rebel against accepted norms.

How do parents deal with above-mentioned conditions? The answer is to deal with the matter, not the person. For instance: no matter how intolerant you are of a messy room, decide if that is a sign of negative resistance. If it is not a matter of life or death, let it be. Perhaps, it is one of their tricks. It is wiser for you to concentrate your energy and time to improve communication skills with your adolescents.

2. Aggressive Attack Method

By the time adolescents use weapons or rude language or become physically violent, they have been unhappy for a long time. They use aggressive behavior because they feel that their position or authority has been threatened. Adolescents might harm someone or break things to show their frustration.

3. Offensive Method

Adolescents use rude languages to express anger. Either they talk non-stop or they use arguments to attract attention. They have no intention of harming anyone, only wishing for sympathy and acceptance.

4. Withdrawal Method

When they do not want to face the cause of their anger, adolescents often uses silence. Parents should not take for granted that silence means your adolescents have already agreed to your opinion. It is quite possible that they just keep the bitterness inside. This condition can easily lead to symptoms called 'Psychosomatic complaints.'

My suggestions—let's grow up together

The best way to prevent anger is to give your adolescents your total attention and tender loving care. Spending time alone with your adolescents will make them feel that they are the most important persons in the world.

Most people express love verbally. However, adolescents are more sensitive to the love expressed through body language. Thus, just saying, "I love you" is not enough. You can use warm glances, physical contact, and time alone to express your love. Bodily contact is the most effective way to restore emotional equilibrium. Whenever an adolescent yells, simply pat him/her on the shoulders gently to keep your communication going. If your adolescent screams at you, you can use eye contact and wait for him/her to calm down. After each outburst, give him/her time to regain calmness and composure. Many parents wrongfully regard a child's silence as disrespectful. Actually, they need time to regain their composure. If you want to be effective in your communication, wait for them to cool off.

The most effective way to control your adolescent's anger is to control your own emotions first. Parents who cannot control their own anger will hurt their adolescent's self-confidence. The adolescents will turn to negative resistance or get into the habit of fighting authority. If parents can look at things positively and treat children's emotions and rights with due respect, their children will grow up to become kind, honest, and decent adults. It will also enhance mutual love and affection.

At times, adolescents feel that they must use language or action to let out steam. Yet, some parents would tell them to shut up or to never allow them to say things like that. Actually, when adolescents use language as a means to show their anger, they will not use an aggressive attack or negative resistance. In other words, they will be less likely to use lies, theft, sex, drug, or alcohol as a means of communication and relief.

Parents can allow adolescents to vent their complaints, but should not allow for anything stronger. If venting turns into cursing and abusive behavior, parents must step in to control the situation. Timing is the key - wait after the explosion to lecture them. For example: When an adolescent screams, "I hate school," do not lecture him/her right away. Wait a few minutes before discussing the reasons why he/she feels that way. After the adolescent has calmed down and able to explain the cause, you can then tell him/her that there are other methods of venting anger.

When a conflict takes place between parents and adolescents, parents should control their own temper. Frequently, when adolescents use annoying and disgusting ways to show their anger, parents' natural reaction would be to raise their voice and give orders, such as, "Take the garbage out right now!" This type of ordering will make adolescent more angry. It is better to say, "Dear, please take the garbage out."

When parents and adolescent are both angry, they should still keep eye contact to show that even though I am not pleased with you, I still care about you. When adolescents are angry, parents should not smile because that may make their child feel despised. Parents should learn not to frown or smile. If an adolescent is unwilling to open up for communication, do NOT nag him/her. Be sure to let him/her know that regardless of his/her behavior or feeling, you love him/her unconditionally. You can tell him/her, "It does not matter if you are happy, sad, or angry. I wish to understand your true feelings."

Even when he/she has exploded, you can encourage and compliment him/her by saying, "I am glad you let me know that you are angry. I am glad that you did not take your anger out on your little sister/brother, or cat/dog. You did not throw things, spit, or hit the wall." Our goal is to effectively help our adolescents deal with anger. Therefore, being skillful is vital. "If you do not improve your grades, how can you be admitted to a good university?" "I know that going to a good university is very important to you. I do not want to see you hurting yourself. How can we solve this problem?" Never say, "You have to get out of this house if you fail your grade again." Saying so will only make the situation worse.

There is one very important lesson in the Bible. It is the manner in which Jesus talked to Peter on the beach after the resurrection. Peter had denied Jesus three times. Yet, Jesus not only unconditionally forgave Peter, but also accepted him and cared for him. Jesus hates sins but he loved Peter, the sinner. Likewise, we love our adolescents. We do not like the mistakes they make, but we can use our love, acceptance, and forgiveness to help them to grow.

To summarize, effective communication must consist the following four C's:

Consistence: The content of your conversation is consistently responsible.

Clarity: You must be clear and easy to understand. There are no tricks up your sleeves.

Completeness: You must have complete mutual understanding—no second-guessing the other party's mind.

Congruence: What is said and what is carried out are the same.

Encouraging words in a conversation

Parents must give adolescents sincere encouragement. Positive encouragement is like a golden apple in silver net. It can bring parents and adolescents closer and forge a special bond. The following are some examples:

1. Son/daughter, I am so glad we can have a meal together to talk.
2. What a capable guy! You have done a great job.
3. Thank you very much for what you have done for your family.
4. Thank you for doing the dishes so quickly.
5. I am proud of you.
6. I am so happy that you study hard.
7. Do you know that you are getting better?
8. I trust you. I believe you.
9. Thank you, my angel.

10. I don't know what I would have done without your help.

11. I admire your persistent willpower.

12. Do not worry, you are doing fine.

13. Right on!

14. Good job! Keep up the good work!

15. You are my best gift from God.

16. Do not feel bad. You will succeed if you try hard.

17. I am grateful. You have tried your best.

18. Child, you add sparkle to my life.

19. Thank you for cleaning/tidying up your room.

20. I am so happy to be with you. You make me happy.

21. It is not easy to concentrate as you do.

22. Your presence gives me inspiration.

23. You are always so thoughtful.

24. Your gentleness gives me lots of encouragement.

25. I am so proud that you always think of others.

26. Wonderful! Your idea helps me a lot.

27. What an insight! I would have never thought of it.

28. Thank you. I have learned a lot from you.

29. We need people like you.

30. Nobody can replace your position in my heart.

10

A Communication Story

The following is a true story, which takes place among a medical doctor, a mother, and an adolescent named Vincent. Vincent is a thirteen years old adolescent who is very healthy and active. His parents got divorced when he was six years old. He lives with his mother who is thirty-eight and is a successful and extremely busy realtor. Mother and son got along peacefully at the beginning. Vincent had maintained good relationships with both his mother and father. However, lately the condition has become tense. Whenever Mother and Vincent are together, they have nothing to talk to each other. They both remain silent for long periods of time. One day when Vincent is sick and taken to his doctor. His doctor notices something is wrong.

The doctor says, "I have known you for a long time. Today you both look unhappy."

Mother replies immediately, "He is so rude, especially during breakfast. He does not respect others. Lately, the school principal telephoned to say that his attitude had gotten bad and he does not study as hard. I am very worried about him. I think his grades would suffer."

Vincent stares at the floor and slowly he says, "It's all her fault. If she does not criticize me all the time, I would feel a lot better."

The doctor deliberately pauses for a couple of minutes for them to cool off. Then he says, "At home do you also argue and then stay silent?"

Both nod their heads.
Mother adds," It has been like this for six months."
Doctor says, "It is quite normal between parents and adolescents. Some adolescents have emotional dilemmas. But, nobody needs to suffer because of it. I hope you can make an appointment to come back so that we can discuss some of the problems, which face adolescents."

Vincent slowly moves his feet and agrees to come back.
Mother says, "I also would like to have such an opportunity."
The doctor's secretary schedules three appointments for them.

The first visit

Both Mother and Vincent describe their feelings. The doctor encourages them to use positive words such as 'concern' instead of negative words such as 'problem' to describe their difficulty.

Doctor, "You come to see me today. What do you expect me to do for you?"

Mother, " Vincent never listens to me. He does not do what I ask him to do."

Doctor, "Vincent, what is your explanation? What is your opinion?"

Vincent, "Mother never understands my feelings. She nags all the time."

The doctor understands the situation so he guides them into a different direction. He allows them to express all of their complaints. Before they leave the office, he asks them to set a goal. The goal is not to blame the other party. And both assume the responsibility to reach the goal and be happy. He explains some of the possible obstacles of reaching the goal. Both Mother and Vincent agreed to try it.

Doctor says, "Today what agreement do you wish to establish?"

Mother, "I wish Vincent will obey me when I ask him to do some chores."

Vincent, "I want everyone happy. I wish she could nicely ask me to do things instead of ordering me."

Doctor, "We have a goal and let's find ways to solve it. How would you achieve your goal?

When you get up in the morning?"

Mother, "I will greet Vincent cheerfully. I will greet him with a smile."

Vincent, "I will be happy and treat her peacefully."

Doctor, "Then how would you achieve these wishes?"

Mother, "We can do homework together; participate in some activities together; play games, share house chores, and show each other affection."

Doctor, "That's wonderful! When will you start?"

Vincent, "From breakfast tomorrow."

Mother, "Start from breakfast!" Finally, the doctor makes some conclusion and both Mother and Vincent agree to carry out doctor's suggestion.

Doctor, "You both want to live peacefully. Can you help each other to achieve this goal?

Starting from breakfast tomorrow?"

Both nod their head simultaneously, saying good-bye to Doctor.

The second visit

Doctor, "Regarding our goal, please tell me what role have you played to keep yourself happy during breakfast?"

Mother, "I cook breakfast and set the table. I wish after the meal, Vincent will automatically clean the table and do the dishes. If I do not have to repeat my requests I would stop nagging."

Vincent, "At the breakfast table I wish to discuss interesting subjects. Otherwise, I will keep silent. No matter what, please do not nag or lecture me."

Doctor encourages them to explore methods of achieving the goal.

Doctor, "What subjects do you want your mother to discuss with you?"

Vincent, "About school and sports. Yesterday, I wanted to talk about my study project on history and the 5 p.m. basketball. I wished she could come home early to see me play. I also hope that she would tell me something about the house she just sold. I just want to have a chance for a good talk."

Doctor concludes, " Vincent, you really want to have a good conversation with your mother."

Vincent, "Yes, Doctor."

Doctor, "That's wonderful! You impress me as a good kid. Mother, can you help him achieve his wish?"

Mother, "Yes, of course. It is really a good turning point for me. From now on, I will happily enjoy my breakfast with my son. "

Doctor, "Let me make sure of your intention you both agree to achieve this goal?"

Mother and Vincent say, "Yes!"

Doctor, "Congratulations! You both have sincere wishes. To achieve our goal, we must use positive methods- live peacefully together, setting up table, washing dishes, discussing interesting topics or stay silent instead of complaining non-stop. Even though your goal can be not achieved in one day, we can accomplish a little at a time. You must both make up your minds to succeed. Is that okay?"

Both nod in agreement, "Bye, Doctor!!"

The Third visit

Doctor, "When did you start having a good communication?"

Mother, "Last Saturday."

Vincent, "I remember it was a week ago."

Doctor, "I am eager to hear every detail! Do you feel different now?"

Mother, "Last Saturday we had a great time. We prepared breakfast together and enjoyed it immensely."

Vincent, "Three weeks ago, without my mother's knowledge, I set up the dining table the night before. When she saw it the next morning, she was so surprised. She was so happy. She thanked me and complimented me. Her changed attitudes made me so happy. That morning, we had a marvelous meal together. After the breakfast,

I had no time to clean up the table because I had to leave. Mother told me that it was okay to wait after dinner to do the dishes."

Doctor, "Mother, on your first visit you said that Vincent never does well what you asked him to do. These past few weeks he obeyed all your orders, what happened?"

Mother, "Once for three days in a row I had to start working early and stayed late. In order to remind him, I listed all the things he must do because I did not have time to discuss with him. However, I called later to leave a message on the answering machine, thanking him for his cooperation."

Doctor, " Vincent, let me ask you the same question. Didn't you say that mother never stops nagging; never listens to you?"

Vincent, "One night after my basket ball game, we went to have some pizza. Mother listened to me explain some details of the game. She was very proud of me. We had a good laugh."

The doctor congratulates them on their improved relationship. He further encourages them to respect, compliment, and help each other. He points out that compliment must be selective, specific, and directional. For example, a father may say to a child, "I admire the gentle voice you use to speak to your mother." "I am so happy to be with you." "You are so thoughtful and considerate, etc."

Mother and Vincent, " Thank you, Doctor. Because of your help, we understand and respect each other. We are growing up together. We feel very loved and adorable. God has given us a loving family."

Conclusion

1. In this story, breakfast is the only chance these two people can talk. Vincent has a lot of extra-curricular activities and schoolwork is getting heavier. Mother has quite a bit of pressure from work. She often works extra hours, making it hard for them to have time together.

2. Vincent is going through adolescence years. He can get annoyed easily. He can be moody.
   He is interested in his friends. He wants to be independent. He desires privacy. On the other hand, he wants mother's company his biggest desire is to be with his mother.

3. Mother was more used to bringing up a little child. She does not understand adolescents' problems. When she faces obstacles and failures, she tries harder, raising her voice and nagging more. The harder she tries, the more Vincent resists.

4. Doctor guides them to shift direction to set a mutual goal. He gives them some methods of solving some possible problems. He advises using honor and positive ways to achieve the set goal. He loans the mother some books regarding adolescence and encourages her to trust a thirteen year old. Finally, there are mutual understanding and respect. When the pressure is lifted, they realize that they can support each other and grow up together in love for the rest of their lives.

11

Keys To Live Peacefully With Adolescents

1. Treat your adolescents with the same respect as you would your friends.

When your children are around twelve years old, you should begin to treat them as young adults in order to reach the ultimate goal of mutual respect and support. This time frame is one of the most beautiful periods of your lives together. You can ride bicycles, climb mountains, fish, cook, and work together. You can go sightseeing or leisurely have a conversation during mealtime. These types of togetherness will give adolescents lasting memories.

Praise and trust are two key ingredients for establishing an adolescent's self-esteem. All adolescents want their parents to listen and understand their feelings. They want to have intimate conversations with you, but not necessarily have the same opinion.

They all have a desire to become intimate friends with their parents. Listening does not obligate you to agree or disagree. Listening also does not mean that you will nor can solve their problems. You should treat your young adult family members with the same manners which you treat your adult friends. Friendship is established by mutual respect and support. Likewise, living peacefully with adolescents does not mean you have to know how to win their favors or gain their love. You just need to treat them with respect as you would with a friend.

2. Avoid "no win" topics.

The worst scenario between parents and adolescents is the constant criticism and pressure given by parents. Parents often demand that their adolescents not deviate from what parents deem to be acceptable behavior. That often means that they demand that their teens follow traditional behavior or mannerisms. While parents mean well, the behavioral parameters that they impose can make the adolescent feel as if they are criticized under a dictatorship.

Parental influence, however, is not the only factor that affects adolescent behavior. Peers can easily influence adolescents. That comes with the territory of growing up. Sometimes teens talk, dress, or act differently from family members. This is a natural response to the changes in their young lives. In essence, it is an indication that they have the desire to become independent. Therefore, the more prudent reaction is not to criticize or attack their fashion, hairstyle, make-up, favorite music, dance, or friends. On the other hand, that is not to say that as a parent you should not put limitations on what is acceptable behavior, dress, and activities. As a parent, one of your responsibilities is to guide your child. The key, however, is to make the teen aware of what is inappropriate without stifling their attempts to spread their wings.

Likewise, you should not dictate their philosophical point of view, the way they spend money, their faith, or their sexual orientation. These slight deviations mean that they are resisting parental authority. These variations also mean that these young adults are beginning to examine and define their identity beyond the one given to them as children. Perhaps, if we can tolerate or work through these differences, we will avoid serious problems such as self-destructive behavior, drug addiction, truancy, and delinquency. One mistake parents often make is criticizing their adolescent's temper, mannerism, and facial expressions without talking things out.

For example, sometimes an adolescent is unable to coherently express his frustration. As a result, he acts out by punching a wall. It is absolutely important for the parent to communicate to the teen that this is an inappropriate reaction and that reprimand is a consequence for such behavior. However, it is equally important for the parent to try to talk with the teen to uncover the underlying frustration. What is difficult for parents of teens is to not automatically react with negative criticism, yelling, or striking. As difficult as it may be, it is important that you refrain from such behavior because it often brings worse reactions by the adolescent. The best solution is for you, the parent, to be a good model yourself from whom he can copy. Intervene only when the adolescent has or is about to cross the line of violating laws or committing serious mistakes that could have a lifetime impact.

3. Let adolescents learn to become responsible members of society.

Adolescents need to ascertain the right path through trials and errors. They will continually refine their judgment via experiences. They will eventually begin to realize that they must take responsibility for their actions. Difficult as it may be, it is best for parents to exercise some self-restraint. Do not intervene in all of your adolescent's matters. Instead, give them positive assurance that you trust their judgment. Parents, however, need to step in when their adolescent is in danger or may commit a crime. During this period it is important for parents to begin relinquishing some responsibility for their teen's life to their teen.

For instance, you want your adolescent to go to school on time. Rather than dictating a time to go to bed, you can explain that she can choose to go to bed no later than a time you determine. However, if she has difficulty getting up in the morning, she must reevaluate her decision and change the time she had chosen to one at which she can get up on time. Another example is the academic responsibility you can give to your teen. Academic grades and homework are closely related. Inform your adolescent that grades and homework are priorities. Let her know that as long as she completes her assignments to the best of her abilities, you will not watch over her as she completes her homework. Let her know the consequence, however, it she does not fulfill her responsibility: If she proves she is unable to do so without supervision, supervise her so that she does her work. As your teen begins learning to accept responsibility and you begin to relinquish it, it is important to communicate that there are consequences to actions and inaction. If they want more freedom and responsibility, they must show that they are both mature and prepared to handle the consequences that come with more autonomy.

During this time, adolescents will begin to realize that the choices they make will have a direct impact on their lives. For example, adolescents will learn that a poor choice of friends may cost them their self-confidence or give them trouble. Adolescents know that if they do not practice hard in sports, they will have pressure from their coach or other team members. Adolescents know that if they spend money carelessly, they will not have any money left at the end of the month, nor have money to buy their favorite things. Adolescents know that if they mistreat friends, they will end up losing them.

Some American parents encourage their youngsters to take jobs during summer to save up for college tuition. This is not necessarily a bad idea. Parents should not give adolescents too much money if they have already earned enough money on their own. The above-mentioned examples show how adolescents can obtain valuable experiences from growing up. When an adolescent asks his parents questions, parents should analyze both positive and negative sides of the question. Let your adolescent make his own choice in order to understand both positive and negative consequences. After analyzing a situation you can tell him, "you do whatever you think is best for you." Before adolescents leave home, they must make plenty of mistakes to learn how to make the right choice. Though they will make mistakes, it is the only way adolescents improve their problem solving skills- coupled with parental encouragement and guidance.

4. Family rules, rewards, and punishments.

The following is a list of rules families with adolescents may choose to adopt:

1). Everyone is obligated to live by family rules. Teens, however, do have some level of privacy in their rooms.

2). No telephone calls after ten o'clock in the evening because late phone calls are rude as they interrupt the recipient's rest and bedtime. Teens must pay for the long-distance phone bills they themselves incurred.

3). No television in a teen's bedroom.

4). Friends are welcome to come home. Prior notice is ideal. However, having a party should have prior approval with the understanding that all guests must also abide by family rules.

5). Adolescents must clean their own rooms as well as wash and iron their own clothes.

6). While it is the teens' responsibility to wear clean clothing and keep up their personal hygiene, parents will demand it when not followed.

7). Parents reserve the right to loan the teen the family car or not. Likewise, parents can decide if adolescents can have the privilege to use bicycles, the computer, the television, or other articles. If an adolescent wants to borrow a car, she must inform the parent where she is going. Adolescents must promise not to drive if intoxicated, not only for their own safety, but also because it is against the law.

When adolescents break family rules, the following are some possible consequences:

1). Take away telephone, television, and car privileges. At this age, standing in a corner or corporal punishment is useless. It only accelerates a bad relationship.

2). If your teen breaks any furniture or decoration, he should repair it or pay for it. He can work to earn the money.

3). If an adolescent messes up the house, she should clean it up.

4). If a teen earns poor grades, parents have the authority to reduce or take away privileges. Parents can also disallow weekend outings.

5). If an adolescent does not return home on agreed upon time and does not telephone to inform the reason of being late, she can be grounded. A good rule of thumb is that it is unwise to ground your adolescents more than a few days. It is foolish and hard to enforce.

5. Family conferences are beneficial when deciding how to carry out family lessons.

Some families participate in a weekly meeting or an after-supper conference as a helpful way to solve problems between parents and children. Some solutions will usually come up during discussion. Family conferences should ideally be a democratic forum. Everybody should be able to voice his opinion. Nobody is allowed to finger point the other's faults. It is a team effort to solve problems. Once the final solution is established, everybody follows it.

6. Use "my feeling" to deal with adolescent's rude and unreasonable attitude.

At times, adolescents will talk back, and sometimes it is laced with sarcasm. Adults want adolescents to express their anger through conversation and use rational manners to discuss challenging topics.

Adults must listen with undivided attention to earn their adolescents' respect. At times when adolescents are emotional, they will become irrational and will verbally attack their parents. When that happens, parents should overlook the inconsequential details. Instead, pay close attention to the cause of the outburst and try to understand them.

Nonetheless, parents should never allow disrespectful name-calling. If they call you "moron" or "dodo" etc, you can tell them your feelings immediately. You can tell him, "Your behavior is inappropriate right now. I cannot treat you like a young adult if you're going to behave childishly and resort to name-calling. When you do that, I lose respect for you because I feel like you're just being hurtful." Or "When you refuse to answer me, I feel slighted." As a parent saying this, you should have an even tone of voice. If she does not listen and continues to use abusive language, it is best for you to walk away. Otherwise, you may unwittingly get into an unnecessary argument and lose your rationality.

7. Argument is not acceptable and useless.

If parents always exercise prudence to avoid using attacking or abusive vocabulary while presenting differing opinions, they will become good role models for adolescents. In case a teen uses rude words to express his opinion, parents must judge what was said rather than the person.

If you can politely and calmly solve a problem, your teen will eventually follow your example and calm down. Then, the conversation can continue after he has cooled off. You do this to show your adolescent that everyone can express a differing opinion calmly and that one can show dissatisfaction without losing his temper. You can also let your adolescents know that rudeness is not allowed in your house.

Every family member should politely welcome all visiting friends of both parents and adolescents. Parents who are honest, sincere, agreeable, and helpful are very good examples for adolescents. Many unpleasant arguments can be averted. If parents dare admit their mistakes and apologize, not only will adolescents will learn to do the same and perhaps reduce the frequency of rude behavior. More importantly, teens will have deep respect for their parents because their parents showed them respect.

12

Discipline of Adolescent

I. What type of adolescent behaviors warrants parental interference?

Parents can overlook the following behaviors:

1. Messy room: Unless the health department wants to inspect the room, leave it alone. General messiness of a bedroom is not deadly. As adolescents grow older, messy habits will gradually disappear.
2. Length and style of hair: Time is on the parents' side. This too is an area that will gradually change over time- usually for the more conservative look.
3. Ear piercing: It is very popular among adolescents now. Discuss with your teen the risks associated with piercing before deciding together what is appropriate.
4. Decibel of music: Allow him to play music within a reasonable

loud limit.

5. Choice of clothing: Let her choose what to wear as along as it is appropriate for her age and the occasion.

6. Fast food: Adolescents love it.

7. Curfews and bedtime: During weekends and holidays, allow them to stay up at night and sleep late in the morning.

8. As long as they finish their schoolwork and family chores, give them some space and freedom. Remember, it is during these years that your teen is learning to develop her interpersonal skills and responsibilities. As she is making well-reasoned decisions, allow her some leeway to expand her horizons. On the other hand, parents should let adolescents know that you care and also have an opinion. Parents should insist that all the rules adopted in family conferences are to be followed by everyone.

II. Parents should interfere with the following behaviors:

1. Messiness beyond her room: Tell your adolescents that picking up after oneself is a family rule that everyone should abide by. Tell your adolescents that you are not their maid and that they are growing up. As a result, they now have more responsibilities. They know how to pick up their own clothes, trash, soft drink can, computers, and books. If they ignore your request after two or three reminders, you withhold allowing them to use their favorite objects- like the computer - for a period of time. If that does not work, a more dramatic approach would be to pile their mess on her beds. You may also use gentle chiding to remind your teen. The key, however, is to enforce the rules thoroughly. Do not give in.

2. Absurd hairstyles: You should be concerned if your adolescents dye their hair odd colors, spike their hair to draw attention, or wear outrageous clothes to parade on the streets. You must discuss these matters with them. Remember you are trying to have a discussion rather than rule with a tirade. Try to understand and search for the cause of this type of behavior- it could be an indication that may be there may be an unseen problem. On the other hand, you should not ridicule your teen about it.

3. Piercing other parts of the body and wearing rings: Besides the ears, you should prohibit your adolescents from piercing other parts of the body, such as nose, tongue, and navel. Tell your teen to respect one's own body because it is the temple of God. Be aware that peers directly influence this type of behavior.

While you must be sure to express your opinion on piercing, try to have an open enough tone of communication that your teen can approach you if he goes ahead and does it without your permission. The reason for this is that parents need to help your teen if there is an infection. Infections require medical attention so you may need to take your teen to a physician. Nose, tongue and navel rings may be removed if there are any health complications.

4. Tattoos: Even though tattoos are very popular nowadays, tell your adolescents that leaving a permanent mark on the body is very unwise and unhealthy. Removing tattoos cost money and it is not easy to do. In addition, tattooing needles are often not sterile. One can get HIV (Human Immunodeficiency Virus) or Hepatitis B from an unclean needle. The chance of getting these diseases is even greater if the tattoo is performed unprofessionally or casually, such as in someone's garage.

Allow your adolescent to use painting colors to draw pictures on his body for a month before deciding on a permanent tattoo. If he still wants tattoo, tell him that after the age of eighteen, he can decide if he still wants it or not. When adolescents are more mature emotionally, they will likely change their views on tattoos.

5. Music and television: Contemporary popular music occasionally contains explicit lyrics full of violence, pornography, isolation, and death. Sometimes, it also encourages using drugs and committing crimes. Some people believe that some of these songs have even inspired murders. It is imperative that you inform your teen that you disapprove of this type of music, which encourages improper or criminal behavior. Tell you teen that you will not provide money for the purchasing these CDs. If possible, try to prevent your adolescents from listening to them. If your teen objects, listen to the music with them and then discuss the content of the lyrics.

Sometimes adolescents defend the music by saying, "I only listen to the rhythm, not the words." That is absurd. Do not believe it. Do not buy this music for them. Contemporary music is not in itself bad; however, it is the message the lyrics convey that is harmful. Encourage your adolescents to listen to contemporary Christian pop music. Most importantly, discuss with your teen the music that they do listen to and try to develop lines of open dialogue.

Another area requiring frank discussion is television. Cable television may have shows that are violent and pornographic. Teens may be fascinated with pornographic shows; however, pornographic movies often contain distorted facts that do not portray real life. Therefore, adolescents can be misguided. Tell your adolescents that the laws are clear. One must be a certain age to purchase and view pornography. Laws were created for a reason: children and teens are not emotionally prepared for understanding certain materials. Consequently, tell your teen that pornography is not allowed in your home. Explain to them that these materials may give them mixed emotions and curiosity mixed with guilt.

Adolescents know parents disapprove of this kind of material. Tell your teen that it is normal to be curious about the opposite sex; however, looking at these pictures may distort their view about sex. If you discover that your adolescent is gay, it is best to take him to a specialist who can help your teen discuss personal feelings, emotions, and fears.

6. Loud music: If the music your teen plays can be heard throughout the whole house and its vibrations can be felt by your neighbor, it is too loud and parents must intervene. Tell her that music should only be heard within the walls of her room. Teach her that excessive loudness will damage eardrums and possibly causing permanent deafness.

7. Daily choice of clothing: Do not allow him to wear clothing with violent and vulgar pictures on it. Do not allow her to wear clothing, which is revealing. Remind your teen that you trust his or her discretion to choose what to wear until you are given reason not to trust it.

8. Finicky eater: Some adolescents use food to fill up the emotional emptiness. Sometimes this leads to binge eating. Binge eating will make someone obese. Lacking love from one's own family can induce binge eating disorders or bulimia. On the other extreme are adolescents who go on a diet to lose too much weight. They are so afraid of being over-weight that they become anorexic. Anorexia nervosa can cause serious complications. Both bulimia nervosa and anorexia nervosa indicate loss of emotional equilibrium. Help from a psychiatrist or psychologist is recommended.

9. Friends with bad habits: If your adolescent has friends who use rude language and act obnoxiously, parents must step in to stop that friendship.

10. Cigarette, alcohol, and drugs: All are signs of bad behavior. Parents not only need to stop their adolescents from using these substances, but also should find help from a specialist.

11. Sexual activity: If you discover that your adolescent is involved in sexual activity, you must stop it. You must also pay special care and try to improve your relationship. You also need assistance from a specialist. Sexual activity is only the tip of the iceberg. More problems are bound to follow.

12. Leaving without saying goodbye: Everybody living under the same roof is obligated to tell other family members where he or she is going, the time of return, and the telephone number to be reached. If you as a parent do this when you leave, this will convey to them that when they do so it does not mean that they are being treated as little children. Instead, they are learning to be responsible people. By example, you will show them that everybody has the duty to treat each other with respect. If an adolescent leaves without saying goodbye and returns a few hours later, it is a sign that there is a problem that he or she cannot tell you.

13. Uncivil language and behavior: Parents and adolescents should treat each other with mutual respect and politely reply to each other. It is permissible for adolescents to be upset when they do not obtain the answer they want or when their parents disagree with them. Nonetheless, an angry retort should not be allowed. Parents should let adolescents know that mutual respect should be maintained at all times and parents will only listen to views and ideas expressed rationally.

In case both sides lose control and get into a heated argument, parents should try to understand their teen's viewpoint and exchange views after everybody calms down. If an adolescent uses very sarcastic language to scold you or your spouse, stop the argument and ask that everyone - including yourself - take a step back. Arguments are not fruitful. You can look at your teen calmly and clearly tell him that you object to his uncivil conduct. Only when he talks calmly should his complaint be discussed.

14. Computer in the home: Thirty-five percent(35%) of American households already have a computer and among those forty-two percent(42%) of households with children own a PC (personal computer). According to the study of Y2000, 60% computers purchased children are key reason of purchase. Therefore, home education is on the fastest growing software segments. It is advised teens should never put any personal information on-line and never agree to a personal get-together with a person they met on-line without parental permission. Adolescents should not send their photography or other identifying information without parental permission. Parents and teen should agree to talk regularly about the people and sites they encounter. He/she should tell parents immediately if they encounter a person or site that makes them feel uncomfortable. Placing family computer in a "high traffic" area of your home will encourage children to share their on-line discoveries—the good and the not so good—with family members. The American Academy of Pediatrics recommends that children should spend less than two hours of total media time per day, including television, film, video games and computer.

13

Formation of Juvenile Delinquency

Signs of juvenile delinquency:

1. Depression, suicidal tendency, excessive drinking, drug addiction, inclination of running away from home.
2. Engaging in risky actions- imprudent actions without worrying about consequences such as reckless driving and unsafe sex.
3. No intimate friends.
4. Totally disregarding schoolwork.
5. Often skipping classes.
6. Displays destructive behavior or explosive temper.
7. Extreme attitude of anti-authority and unwillingness to cooperate with family members.
8. Causing family to break down or disintegrate.
9. Needing constant criticism and punishment.

Causes of formation of juvenile delinquent

1. Malfunction of family

From the moment of birth, a child imitates every action of his family members. He will copy the intonation of speech and the style of walking, even the thinking process. If family members regard shoplifting, drinking, and using drugs as common behaviors, a child will subconsciously accept the same concept. He will do the same when he grows up.

According to experts, it is noted that seventy-five percent (75%) of what a child does is taught by parents. Having been given the training and education opportunity or not, a child learns to accept or refuse wrongful things. If parents fail to guide completely and a child is uncertain of right or wrong, even without a model to emulate, there is still a twenty-five percent (25%) chance, that a child will decide what to do by him based on his personality.

2. Poor relationship with parents, or rigid parental discipline

Some parents think that corporal punishment will achieve the goal of warning, guidance, and obedience. However, more frequently the result is just the opposite. Even if a child tolerates beating, he keeps his anger inside. As his wrath accumulates, he will show his defiant behavior. Because he has so much pain, so much shame, feels so despised by his parents, and so unloved, he will seek love and care outside. Because his heart is shadowed by beating and violence, he will easily get into fights with schoolmates. When teachers tell him he cannot fight with others, he is not convinced. If his parents can hit him, why can he not hit other kids?

One teenager pours some paint on a new car, deep inside of his heart he knows that he will be punished for it, but he would not know why. A child asks his father the time for dinner. The father says, "Don't bother me. Go play somewhere else." In a single parent family a mother is often seen lying on a couch in drinking stupor. When she wakes up from her drunkenness, she beats up her children. Of course children in these kinds of families would wish to leave to go somewhere they can find solace. Therefore, using love to raise children will greatly reduce the chance of them turning bad.

3. Lacking discipline

Parents are careless- they don't care what their children do. They let children do anything they want. It is not that parents do not love their children; it is because they have a very loose concept of discipline. If the parents' attitude is, "I have no control over them. I don't know what to do, when the children get into trouble, then children would assume parents' discipline is correct. The children will continue to do whatever they wish, not differentiating right from wrong. Therefore, parents should apply brakes to control their children. Though children may not totally obey, at least in their hearts, they know their parents would not agree.

4. Two sets of discipline

A child does something wrong. His father takes away his bicycle privilege for a week. Next day the child whines and nags his mother to let him ride the bike. Mother is tired of nagging. She lets him ride the bike. The child rides his bike knowing fully well that his father disapproves of it. This type of inconsistent discipline will make an adolescent take advantage of (and despise) his parents. If grandparents and parents have different sets of discipline, the situation can be worse.

5. Rejection by parents

Some parents do not understand a child's feelings. They repeatedly say they love him. Yet, when an adolescent tells them his secrets, parents show distrust, making him feel that they do not really care. He cannot accept them. Parents often overlook the behavioral signals sent of by the adolescent. Parents will come to a rude awakening one-day when problems occur. Parents at last understand the meaning of the previously sent behavioral signals.

6. Excessive love of parents

It is not that parents do not care. It is that parents care so much that they spoil the child. Parents always do as the child says. They never say, "No." They go along with everything the child does, including staying out all night. The fact is most of the serious problems take place during the time an adolescent stays out late. Discipline too strict and too loose is two extremes. Both extremes produce juvenile delinquents.

7. Parents are at discord

Some parents argue, quarrel, even fight in front of a child. The child cannot get involved. He cannot take sides. Therefore, he is averse to staying home because every time he is home the same old scene appears. Thus, it is advisable to parents that if they need to argue, do it when their adolescent is not home.

8. Violence at home

When a father violently beats up a child or a mother, it will leave a deep scar in the soul of an adolescent. He will assume parents really do not love him. When he sees his father, he sees violence. This type of violence will affect the future marriage life of the adolescent. He will presume that violence is an acceptable conduct and a means of solving problems.

9. Break down of a family

The following is an observation and feelings of an adolescent:

During dinnertime at my house, my father always eats by himself in the living room. He eats and watches his favorite boxing on television. My mother, my sister, and I sit at the table, eating quietly. To me, this is an incomplete family, a broken family.

My uncle's family is a happy one. They have three children. Their dinner is accompanied by laughter. They play baseball together. They always act together. It is not like that in my house. My father always says, "I am too busy to play baseball with you!" When I lived with my grandparents, every year we had summer vacation together. My sister had to stay home. She did not have any vacation because my parents did not give her time. What kind of family is this? It is only a group of people living under the same roof! When I pass them in the living room, they never say, "Good morning" to me or greet me in any manner. When I need them, they will not spend time with me, either. We never discuss anything. I know we are only living within the same space of a house.

My aunt also has a nice family. They take vacation together and eat together. I have never seen them argue. When students have to stay after school and my aunt will come to pick my cousins, they always have so much to talk about! My aunt will ask them for the interesting things during school. I really admire them. I wish my parents were like that.

14

Children of single parents

I t is a common phenomenon to have families with single parents when statistics shows that as high as fifty percent (50%) of marriages in the United States, twenty to twenty-five percent (20%-25%) in Taiwan, thirty percent (30%) in Hong Kong and ten to fifteen percent (10%-15%) in China end in devoice. Marrying too young (before the age of twenty) is the major reason of divorce. When a couple marries young, there is no sufficient time to understand each other's personality, life style, or value standard. Difficulty of adjusting to each other often leads to the breakup of a marriage.

Annual divorce in the United States produces one hundred thousand unhappy ex-spouses and one million children with single parents. In Taiwan, the number is forty thousand unhappy ex-spouses and fifty thousand children. Society and churches need to sympathize and help solve the problems associated with single-parent families.

Premature death of one spouse is another factor, which creates families with one parent to take care of children alone.

According to the recent census only twenty-six percent (26%) of American children live with both parents under the same roof. Only eight percent (8%) of children have fathers who work while mothers stay as homemakers. However, there are fifty percent (50%) of children raised by single parents and while eighty percent (80%) of them are raised by mothers. Two years after divorce, fifty percent (50%) of fathers have little contact with their children. From the above statistics, divorce has greater impact on children's emotional growth than the pain parents suffer.

The statistics also show that the first year after the divorce the income of families with single-mothers suffer a great reduction- up to fifty-eight percent (58%). In the divorce settlement only fifty percent (50%) of fathers agree to pay child support. Out of them only fifty percent (50%) actually pay. Only those single parent families with regular child support can maintain the same level of living standard. Families without child support often suffer such financial stress that other complications follow.

Most divorces take place when children are between the ages of two and eight. And this is the critical period of time when children most need their parents to guide them on sex orientation and personality formation. No wonder children of divorced parents often suffer some deviation of personality growth and sexual development. Their impression and concept of the opposite sex are often distorted.

1. Children's emotional reaction to divorce

Fear: When children see their parents fight; don't get along; use bad body language; or give each other ugly stares, a great fear will grip the children's heart. How can I continue to live? What will my future be? These unknown create a great deal of fear in their hearts.

Guilt: A child will wonder if he is the reason his parents quarrel. Did they break up because I was bad? Divorce can create a great deal of guilt and self-accusation in a child's heart.

Grief: The pain following the divorce will make a child fall into a long period of grief. He will have a pessimistic view on his future and every thing around him.

Anger: Children in a divorce will get very mad at their parents. They can't forgive their parents for not getting along. They are also mad at relatives and friends. They can't accept any advice or encouragement because they figure divorce is the death of a marriage and the breakup of a family. There is no more help.

2. Children's initial reaction to divorce—Children's reactions immediately after the divorce differ by age group:

Between two and a half to four years old:

Children of this group will become withdrawn; negative; non-cooperative, loss of appetite, insomnia, inactive, and loss of interested in living.

Between three and half to five years old:

Children of this group may display more aggressive behaviors. They may have temper tantrum, become unreasonable and act contrary to everyone, or revert to baby-like behavior. One-third of children may take a year for these symptoms to surface. A year after the divorce, sixty percent (60%) of young children's behaviors regress. Some children may gradually develop depression and immature behaviors. They become quiet and sorrowful, pessimistic, blaming everything around him. In general, girls suffer more from divorce than boys do.

Between seven and adolescence years:

Children of this age group usually lose emotional equilibrium and suffer some damage to their personalities. Self-image is tarnished. It is awkward to be caught between father and mother. They suppress their sorrow in the subconscious.

After certain period of suppression, their spirit returns only to be followed by many physical symptoms such as headache, stomach pain, worsening of asthma, etc. Noticeably, fifty percent (50%) of children suffer academically grades drop.

3. An adolescent's response to parents' divorce

A typical adolescent will feel abandoned and lost. He/she will worry about financial condition. Can I go to college? Will my marriage be like my parents'? Boys may get into illegal drugs and theft. Girls may get into drugs and become promiscuous.

Some parents use every possible means to fight for custody. Children get caught in the middle, unable to express his position. It is advisable that the custodial parent and children do not move out of the house immediately following the divorce settlement because it will be more difficult adjusting to a new environment and challenge. It usually takes two to seven years for a single parent to adjust to the new role and take on the duties of single-parenthood successfully.

A single parent needs to play a double role of being a dad and a mom. That she needs to help her adolescent cope with all kinds of adversities besides providing a safe and secure home commends everybody's sympathy. Only those who have experienced it would understand how difficult it is. At times a custodial parent would wonder if she has fulfilled her duty. Particularly if she needs to work long hours for a meager salary, she would wonder if she is going to make it.

However, the answer is affirmatively YES! The heavenly Father is the Lord who loves you and understands you. He will not leave you alone. As long as you let Him hold your hand, He will guide you through your life. He is God of compassion and cares for the lonely and the sorrowful.

One day when you look back, you will realize faith has given you tremendous strength. It is so precious and powerful. Without being fully aware of it, you have accomplished the duties of God has entrusted you. If you need any help from Single Parent Association you may dial 1-800-a Family. They will help all parents who ask for it.

The following is a list of guidelines for your reference:

1). **Love your child:** However, be prudent about limits- do not over-indulge. If you pamper too much, your child may get spoiled. If you don't pay enough attention, your child may go off the right path. There is a happy medium.

2). **Pray without ceasing.** Cast your burden to the Lord because He cares for you. He will listen to your prayer and comfort you. He will give you strength and courage. He will give you abundant love and discernment. Prayer will move God's hand to do miracles. Pray for your children also. Grow with them in love. The power of prayer is beyond human comprehension. Prayer brings love. Love brings power to change everyone.

3). **Get assistance from friends.** A single parent may discover that friends seem to desert her after the divorce. Many people avoid contact with divorced families because they more or less feel that divorce can be contagious. They do not want their families to be inflicted, so they avoid contact with a divorced parent or a remarried couple. In addition to the above circumstances mentioned, a single parent often gets into a deep financial struggle for which even friends are futile. Regardless of the difficult conditions, all single parents must give children reassurance that parents' unending love is unconditional.

4). **Try to keep your emotional balance.** Use calm attitude to treat your adolescent. Single parent is able to maintain a peaceful family full of love, support, and understanding. Use the guidelines given in the Bible to bring up your children.

4. Image problem of children of divorced families

Children two to six need both parents to nourish. It is a period of time when children need both parents' guidance to form male/female image and identity.

If his mother alone raises a boy, he is more likely to be lacking father's male image. Thus, he will desire some male figure to fill his void. If this void is left unfilled, he may have homosexual tendency during adolescence. What he wants is not sexual satisfaction but fatherly love. Only when he and the admired male figure have physical contact will they become gay lovers. On the contrary, when his craving for father's love is not satisfied, he might seek a female to prove his masculinity and to elevate his pride.

If her father alone raises a girl, she will have less opportunity to have contact with females. She will lack her mother's female image. Thus during the growth processes, he will desire some female figure to fill her void. During adolescence, she will respect some admired females. If she and an admired female have physical contact, she will develop a lesbian tendency. If she has had bad dating experience with males, she very likely will become lesbian relationship. On the contrary, when she lacks a female image or when her image is damaged, she could become promiscuous to prove that she is a very attractive female in order to satisfy her emotional needs.

One other end of the pendulum, some adolescence raised by single-parents refuse to accept their true sexes- he does not want to be a boy and she does not want to be a girl. And the single parent allows them to wear clothing of the opposite sex. Emotionally they are the opposite sex of what they are born with. A specialist must treat this type of problem.

Not all children of single parent families turn out into one of the above-mentioned examples because most boys still receive a certain degree of male figure to fill his void and receive fatherly nurturing. Likewise, most girls have certain female figure to fill her void and receive the nurturing of a motherly figure.

Raising children take both parents. When single parents find themselves assuming the responsibilities of raising their children alone, they often sink into a helpless condition. Life has completely changed. Emotionally they may become very dependent on their children. Sometimes, they regard their children as their spouse replacement. They lose clear sense of direction. Some single parents are full of guilt. They want to make up to the children. Therefore, they spend a great deal of time with their children and let them have anything they ask. This will lead children to take advantage of parents and be spoiled. On the other side of the extreme are some single parents who regard their children as their only hope.

They think that they must not fail. Therefore, they interfere with everything children do. These single parents are so strict that their children are not given by free space, making the children fiercely resentful.

15

How much do you know about tobacco, liquor and drugs?

Three environmental factors affect today's teen-agers enormously: family, schools, and friends. Naturally, teens demand more and more autonomy and try to separate from family ties, because they feel they are grown up and are able make their own decisions. On the other hand, teens seek association with friends of the same caliber. The impact from the friends becomes tremendous. In today' s society, teens are exposed to drugs, and sex, which make them more vulnerable to cope with the situations. As a result of these challenges, teens are facing more difficulty in life.

Alcohol causes more deaths among adolescents than any other substance. About forty percent (40%) of all deaths in sixteen to twenty-years-old result from motor-vehicle crashes, and half of these are alcohol related.

According to the American statistical data of 1997, teen death existed and 40% of death was related to the use of alcohol as shown in the graph below.

Statistics of death (15-24 years of age)

Cause of death	Rate/100,100	Number	Alcohol related
Accident	60.0	25,000	40%
Traffic accident	30.0	15,000	45%
Homicide	13.0	5,500	30%
Suicide	12.5	5,000	20%

Surprisingly, among ninety one percent (91%) of high school graduates confessed that they consumed alcohol in their life. Even five percent (5%) of them were classified as alcoholic, because of their frequent drinking habit. Furthermore, fifty percent (50%) of high school graduates admitted that they used marijuana in their lifetime and 4% of high school students used marijuana daily.

As far as smoking, twenty five percent (25%) of high school students abused cigarettes in 1975. That percentage dropped to nineteen percent (19%) in 1986, and rose up to seventy percent (70%) in 2001. But in the last five years, tobacco companies have tried to promote smoking and targeted the youth population in their advertising. As a result, the smoking age group is younger than before. If a teen becomes addicted to smoking before the age of 18 years, the tobacco company has a permanent customer.

Three drugs are considered the gateway of drug addiction: alcohol, tobacco, and marijuana. Once teen steps into drug usage, he gets trapped and begins using more often. Later on, he will become addicted. Studies have shown drug users are younger than ever before. Why does that happen?

There are two factors involved: psychological and biological factors. If there is yet another factor superimposed, susceptibility to drug abuse will worsen.

Psycho-social factors:

1. Low self-esteem.
2. No sense of belonging.
3. High need for social approval.
4. Disrupted relation with family members.
5. Poor communications, poor adjustment abilities and skills.
6. No satisfaction.
7. Inadequacy to accept the consequences of the their actions.

Biological factors:

1. Genetic factor
2. Parental influence
3. Peer group pressure
4. Social-cultural influence and difference in their value system.

Besides the above two sets of factors, the main issue is the personality of the youth. He/she has the absolute determination to decide for himself/herself how to face the challenge. However, fifty percent (50%) of personality formation is formed in the first 3 years of life and this is modulated from parents and family. The rest of fifty percent (50%) gradually develops from the impact of society, culture and friends. Who then are more vulnerable to the drug abuse? The following are the risk factors:

1. Family factors: parents with drinking problem will often do nothing about it until they see the same problem in their offspring.
2. Other family factors: parents, siblings who have history of drinking and drug usage. For example, the adolescent may complain: "Why are you so upset about my drinking, when you are drinking?"
3. Peer group pressure: curiosity, conformity, and fear of being different.
4. Personality: loss of self-confidence, variable and weak ego is prone to get involved drugs.
5. Persons who have abnormal psychological and mental disorder are more involved in drugs usage.

The family factor is very important factor. Parental attitude toward drinking, poor raport with teens, and the history of parental alcohol or drugs usage, is the cornerstone for determining the adolescent's susceptibility to abuse. Parental condonation of drug use also increases the likelihood of the drug abuse among adolescence. Parents serve as models for their adolescent children. Children whose parents smoke, drink or abuse drugs are more likely to do so than those whose parents do not. Thus, parental attitude and behaviors regarding the use of substances at home may influence the development of attitude and beliefs regarding drugs and alcohol.

Three parental factors can predict the teen's initiation into drug use: the parent's own drug-using behavior, parental attitude about drugs, and parent-teen interactions.

THE GATEWAY DRUGS: TOBACCO, ALCOHOL, MARIJUANA AND INHALANTS

Tobacco—the smoking gun

Tobacco was initially smoked or taken as snuff by the native North and South Americans for centuries and was introduced in Europe as a medical herb in the 16th century. Then the use of tobacco became a widespread social event and it has remained so today. In 19th century, most of the tobacco use in America was a chewable tobacco: few people smoked. However, since the "roaring 20s" smoking has taken over chewing and cigarette smoking became a national habit after the veterans returned from World War II. As the health dangers of smoking are documented, we begin to see a return to the use of chewable or smokeless tobacco.

The active ingredient of cigarette smoke and chewed or snorted tobacco is nicotine. The alkaloid is well absorbed in the lungs by inhalation or through the mucous membrane of mouth and nose. Nicotine is deactivated in the liver and excreted by the kidney and is highly toxic. Symptoms of low-level poisoning- dizziness, nausea, and generalized weakness- are frequently noticed by the beginning of smoking. A toxic overdose can lead to tremor, convulsion, and paralysis of respiratory muscle and death. Even though the nicotine acts to shift the brain wave into an arousal pattern, most smokers claim the net effect is relaxation and relief of tension. Another toxic component of cigarette smoke is carbon monoxide which is responsible for the dispense on exertion and affect the fetus through the placenta. The tars and other carcinogens from tobacco are responsible for the malignancies. Infant and young children of smoking parents are at increased risk for serious respiratory illness such as pneumonia and bronchitis.

Most of teens smoke because of curiosity, which could be from the influence from parents, brothers, and friends who smoke. The girls tend to have higher ratio of involving smoking. Because smoking can be the way of expressing independence and symbol of anti-authority, there is 10-15 times higher chance to contract lung cancer after 15 to 20 years of smoking. Second hand smoke is also a troublemaker of lung problem.

The most effective treatment for cigarette smoking is to prevent the onset of behavior through the peer counselor targeting early adolescence. Nicotine patch, acupuncture, and chewing gum may be helpful. Many people had tried so many times to abstain smoking, but in vain. However, many people quit smoking after they have experienced life transformation from accepting Jesus as their personal Savior. Because of the new life providing them peace, joy, and an everlasting spiritual satisfaction, they are able to overcome the emotional tobacco dependence.

Alcohol—the most dangerous gateway drug

Besides caffeine many people use alcohol. Humans have consumed alcohol beverages since 6,400 BC. In 1839, England imposed a penalty for selling spirit to persons under the age of 16 years, while in the various states of the U.S.A.; the legal drinking age continues to fluctuate between 18 and 21 years. Despite of the effect to regulate teenage drinkers, enormous numbers of adolescents consume alcohol.

Recent study from Columbia University indicated that among high school students, eighty-one percent (81%) students drank alcohol, seventy percent (7%) smoked cigarette, and forty-seven percent (47%) experienced marijuana.

In the past, men were more likely to drink than women, but at least in the adolescent population, this difference seems to be lessening. The majority of girls, who have the drinking habit, tend to have a psychological imbalance, psychosomatic disorder or are from families whose parents having less education. In addition, family life with alcoholic parents is often disruptive and sometimes abuse and can lead to a wide variety of problem behavior in adolescent children, including alcohol and drug abuse.

Alcohol (Ethyl Alcohol C2H5OH) is produced by fermentation of the starch or sugar in various fruits and grains by the action of yeast. Alcohol is consumed in the form of beer, made from barley and hops and containing approximately five percent (5%) alcohol. Wine made from grapes, approximately fifteen percent (15%) alcohol; and spirits or hard liquor (Scotch, RUM Vodks, Gin) distilled from barley, corn or sugar can, approximately forty-five percent (45%).

Alcohol is quickly and effectively absorbed from the gastrointestinal tract and requires no digestion. The rate of absorption depends on the concentration of alcohol, the amount and type of food in the stomach and whether or not the liquid is carbonated. Eating foods containing fat and /or protein before or while drinking alcohol will help to delay absorption.

The effect of alcohol is noticed approximately 10 minutes after consumption and will peak at approximately 40-60 minutes after the ingestion. The alcohol will remain unchanged in blood, lungs or kidneys until metabolized by the liver. If an individual consumes at a faster rate than it can be metabolized, the blood alcohol concentrate will rise. The initial metabolic product is acetaldehyde, which plays a control role in alcohol toxicity. Therefore, the tolerance is explained by the induction of enzymes in the liver, which allows faster metabolism of the drugs, and some by brain tolerance, an adaptation to the neuropsychological effects of alcohol. The physical dependence develops after years of heavy consumption, after which abstinence can result in delirium tremors, a withdrawal syndrome that can cause seizures and death.

Alcohol is a central nervous system depressant. At the high level, it leads to respiratory depression, arrest and death. At low level, alcohol impairs regulatory and inhibitory central mechanism in the brain. Complex and poorly learned behaviors, such as driving in young people, are impaired. Anxiety is reduced, judgment is poor; and attention, short- term memory, and thought processing are impaired. As the blood level rises, motor coordination becomes impaired, and reaction time becomes quite prolonged. If drinking continues a stupor, coma, or death can occur.

Alcohol related motor vehicle accidents are the leading cause of death for 15- 24 years-old Americans, either as drinkers or passengers. Two cans of beer will raise the blood level to the legal inhibition level (0.08- 0.10). The following are the symptoms, which are related to the blood alcohol level:

Blood alcohol level

0.05%	high feeling, anxiety reduced, excited.
0.2%	markedly intoxicated.
0.3%	stupor, coma.
0.5%	death

Because of alcohol in the lungs is quite compatible with blood alcohol level, the breath test to check the alcohol level is quite accurate. You should not drive if your blood level is 0.08- 0.11%, which is very easy to obtain that level by merely drink two cans (12oz/bottle) of beer.

The adolescent may complain to the parents "Why are you so upset about my drinking, when you drink also?" In this case, the adolescent may need to be reminded that it is legal for adult to drink. However, for the fairness to the adolescents, the parents should acknowledge that although it is legal for adult to drink, even adults who drink to excess need help. The Bible does not prohibit drinking, but the Bible emphasizes we should not be drunk. In order to set a good example for the teens, it may be wise to abstain from alcohol beverage.

For more information about alcohol prevention and treatment, call, read or visit:

Make a Different: Talk to Your Child About Alcohol
U.S. Department of Health and Human Service.
Available from the National Institute on Alcohol Abuse and Alcoholism at www.niaaa.nih.gov or by calling 1-800-487-4889

Marijuana—inhaled intellectual impairment

In America, over 50 million people have tried marijuana (THC, Pot, Weed, Hash, Grass). Among high school seniors in the U.S.A., over half have used the drug at least once in their lifetime with approximately 47% reporting use annually, making marijuana the most common illicit drug chosen by adolescents. It is quite astonishing, 4% of high school seniors use it daily. Marijuana is obtained from the hemp plant (Cannabis Sativa). The pharmacological effects are related to the concentration of delta-9-tetrahydrocannabinol (THC) and other cannabinoids that are found in the leaves and flowering shoots.

Effects begin within seconds to minutes after inhalation of the smoking or within 30-60 minutes following oral ingestion. The smoking routes are more rapidly and directly absorbed from the lungs to the brain and other organs than through the oral or injected routes. Although the initially high blood level of THC falls rapidly over the first 30 minutes, further elimination occurs more slowly, which may take 19 hours for one half of the initial level to disappear. Repeated use may result in an accumulation of cannabinoids, as blood levels do not accurately reflect concentrations present in the brain or other organs because the cannabinoid are readily distributed into tissues through the body. This is quite different from alcohol or caffeine and nicotine, which are rapidly metabolized and completely eliminated.

The main effect of marijuana is the stimulation of the central nervous system: the person will increase visual, auditory and taste perception as well as increased concentration, elevated blood pressure, emotional relaxation, and sharp vision. Therefore, musicians, painters, and sportsmen like to take marijuana because of the enhancement of longer physical excitement.

But marijuana has a major effect on performance of task related to coordination: lack of hand steadiness and decrease in postural stability manifested by an increase in body sway. The chronic users may develop: A-motivational syndrome, which consists of loss of energy, apathy, absence of ambition, inability to carry long-term plan, problem of concentration, loss of effectiveness, and impaired memory.

Therefore, the deleterious effects of marijuana are behavioral rather than somatic. The withdrawal symptoms include irritability, agitation, insomnia and may peak at 30 hours after discontinuing marijuana use, and symptoms may take three to four days to disappear. If you take marijuana four times a week for six months or more, the male hormone may be reduced and sperm production will be slowing down. Your height and growth development may be affected also.

BEYOND THE GATEWAY- DEAD-END DRUGS

Cocaine—the fast track downhill

Cocaine use by adolescents has increased dramatically in the recent years. A national survey from high school seniors revealed that cocaine use increased from nine percent (9%) in the class of 1975 to one hundred and seventy-three percent (173%) in the class of 1986. Lifetime or "ever use" in high school seniors were seventeen percent (17%) in 1985, nine point four (9.4%) in 1990, five point nine percent (5.9%) in 1994 and eight point seven percent (8.7%) in 1997. The growing popularity of cocaine use among adolescents can be attributed to a combination of several major factors: (1) Increased use among adults, including its use by famous athletes, entertainers, business executives, and professionals who serve as role models for youngsters of all ages; (2) the perpetuation of cocaine's image as a chic, upper-class, non- addictive, relatively harmless, intoxicant which produces a sensational "high"; (3) the abundance of cocaine supplies, and at reduced prices, which make the drug more accessible; and (4) the appearance of "crack" on the illicit drug market and at a price almost any teenager can afford.

Cocaine hydrochloride powder is the most popular form of cocaine in the USA.

It is a white, crystalline substance sold on the illicit drug market in units of a gram, ranging in price from $75 to $100 per gram. The cocaine powder can be purchased in ounce, quarter or eight. Crack is sold in a very small dosage units of ready-to-smoke "rock' that can cost as little as $5 or $1 each which is within financial reach of any teenager. Cocaine can be absorbed into the blood stream through nasal inhalation or "snorting" and intravenous injection. When cocaine and heroin are mixed together in the same syringe, the drug combination is known as a "speedball". The smokable form of the drug is known as freebase or "crack". Smoking of cocaine generates an instanteous and extremely intense euphoria or "rush". The "high" is extremely pleasurable, but short-lived (half life 1 hours), leading to a pattern of repeated dosing at short intervals in order to maintain the desired mood state. As usage becomes regular and intensified, the brief euphoria is followed immediately by an unpleasant rebound dysphoria, or "crash". That is why the user desires to have an immediately return to the euphoria state. Therefore, the greatest danger is it has high addiction potential.

The most common medical problems from cocaine use are usually related to the route of drug administration. Intranasal users may experience rhinorrhea, sinus headache, nasal congestion and nasal bleeding. Chronic freebase smokers may have chest congestion, wheezing, and sore throat from inhaling the hot cocaine vapors. Intravenous users tend to experience the most serious drug-related medical problems, which results from the use of un-sterile needle, including hepatitis, abscess at the injection sites, endocarditis, and exposure to AIDS.

The most obvious and severe consequences of chronic cocaine usage are behavioral, psychological, and social dysfunction. Cocaine abuse during pregnancy has been associated with increased spontaneous abortion, stillbirth and congenital malformations.

Amphetamine—the fast track downhill

Amphetamines were first used in the USA during the early 1950s. They were prescribed for obesity, mild depression, attention deficit, and hyperkinesis.

Today, they are considered to have a high potential for abuse and considered as a controlled drug.

Street names include "Speed," "Splash," and "Uppers," "Black beauties" "BAM", "Mollies." and "Bennies". The proportion of high school seniors who used amphetamines dropped from 15% to 7%

between 1976 and 1982; however, the rate has remained fairly constant since that time, and it rose up to seventeen percent (17%) in 1997. At least once by twenty-three percent (23%) of high school seniors have used amphetamines at least once.

Within 30 minutes of oral ingestion or five minutes following subcutaneous injection, amphetamines begin to exert its effect. The effects begin almost instantly after intravenous administration, and they are extremely intense. Amphetamines may result in an initial "rush" or feeling of extreme exhilaration that are followed by a more sustained period of euphoria with greater ability to concentrate, wakefulness, depressed appetite, self-confidence, and excitement.

Mild amphetamine toxicity includes restlessness, irritability, insomnia, tremor, hyper-reflexes, dilated pupils, and flushing. With increased dosage, the adolescent will experience confusion, hypertension, tachypnea, and low-grade fever. With more severe toxicity, delirium, hypertensive crisis, seizure, coma and even death are possible.

The other amphetamine derivative- Methamphetamine (Speed, Ice, Chalk, Meth, Crystal, Crank, Fire, Glass, Poor-man's coke) was documented as use of ephedrine in China 5,000 years ago. It was recognized for its stimulant, appetite suppressant and bronchodilator properties. However, it is a toxic, addictive stimulant that affects many areas of the central nervous system. Diverse groups, including young adults who attend Raves in many regions of the country, are using it, and it has reached an epidemic level. Methamphetamine can be smoked, snorted, injected, or orally ingested and is associated with serious health consequences, including memory loss, aggression, violence, psychotic behavior, and potential cardiac and neurological damage. It is relatively cheap and gives users a more sustained high than cocaine. The teenagers use this drug to boost mood and self-confidence, suppress appetite to lose weight, and enhance sexual experience.

Another form of amphetamine "Methylenedioxymethamphetamine (MDMA) (Ecstasy, XTC, Adam, Clarity, Lover's Speed) is enabling to users to dance for extended periods and is similar to the stimulant amphetamine and the hallucinogen mescaline.

Phencyclidine (PCP)—checking out of reality

Phencyclidine (PCP, Angel dust) is an extraordinarily dangerous hallucinogen. It can induce profound alterations of all sensory perceptions (as sight, sound, touch, smell, and taste), essentially jerking its users far from normal consciousness. Agitated PCP users may demonstrate incredible strength oneself and no apparent sensation of pain, making him extremely dangerous to those who might try to restrain him.

The consequences of large doses of PCP can result in heart failure, seizure, coma, and lethal stroke. The frequent users may risk direct brain damage, leading to alterations of speech, loss of memory and intellectual functions, and psychosis. PCP can be swallowed or smoked (sprayed onto tobacco or marijuana) or injected with tragic result.

LSD (Lysergic acid diethylamide)—out of reality of life

LSD, a faded relic of the psychedelic sixties, has come back again.

Small amounts of LSD swallowed or licked off paper can produce intense exhilarating or terrifying hallucinations. Its effects are somatic (physical effects), perceptual (altered changes in vision and hearing) and psychic effects (sensorial changes).

The worst of the "bad trip" can bring on profound anxiety, panic, confusion, or self-destructive behavior, such as jumping off a building or stepping in front of oncoming traffic.

Heroin—painkiller with a hook

Heroin, one of the opiates, is a white, bitter, crystalline powder. When obtained by the users, it is usually mixed with lactose, which serves as a filler to dilute the opiate. The daily use by the high school student is less than one percent (1%). Because the opiate abuse and addiction are associated with dropping out of school, these teenagers would not be detected by an in-school survey. However, the intravenous drug abuse has become a matter of great concern in view of the relationship between such activity and AIDS.

Heroin can be administrated via intranasal route or snorting, skin-popping and intravenous route. They all produce intense effects immediately or within 15 minutes. Heroin will induce euphoria, pain control and forgetting all the unpleasant feelings. There is a high incidence of addiction after repeated uses. Once addiction occurs, without the constant heroin, a user goes through withdrawal symptoms (so called "cold turkey"). These include perspiration, vomiting, diarrhea, and muscle spasm. Pregnant woman who uses heroin may often have premature, still birth or low birth weight newborns.

Volatile Substances—cheap and dangerous thrills

Inhaling volatile gases: Such as nitrous oxide or ether for mind-altering effects was quite popular among adults in the nineteenth century. However, abuse of inhalants by adolescents became a concern in USA in the early 1960, with the epidemic of glue sniffing among children and young teenagers. Because of the low price, and easy obtainability from the market, the teenagers have loved volatile substances.

Airplane glue: It was quite popular during 1960 - 1970 in the USA. However, it is coming back to the adolescent society. The main chemical substance is toluene which can be found in paints, lacquer thinners, aerosols used as propellants for deodorants, type-writer correction fluid, household and model glues. After the inhalation, the person may experience total relaxation, and euphoria, which may last for about two hours. The repeated use of the glue will eventually develop dependence and chronic intoxication. Excessive inhalation may cause swelling of brain, lungs, heart muscle, and hematuria as well as kidney failure.

Gasoline sniffing: It was quite popular in the remote urban areas. There will be a period of excitement, followed by euphoria after the inhalation. Long-term usage of the gasoline sniffing will cause irreversible brain damage, bone marrow failure (caused by benzene) and lead poisoning.

Aerosol products: The main ingredient is haloggenated hydrocarbons (freon), which can be found in hair spray, deodorant, and cocktail spy. Sudden death has been reported from the inhalation of a large quantity. This death is thought to be due to cardiac arrhythmia resulting from sensitization of the heart to epinephrine.

Volatile nitrite: It became popular in 1970s among male homosexuals. And it has been used in conjunction with a sexual experience of heterosexual intercourse.

Ketamine

Ketamine (Special K, K, Vitamin K, Cat Valium) was initially used as anesthetic for cats and dogs. It is also used as a clinical anesthetic in human beings. In February 1998, the U.S. Drug Enforcement Administration warned that Ketamine has been popular among the American sub-cultural parties such as Raves parties and marathon dancers. Ketamine has been abused as a stimulant, which almost substitutes heroin and speed. It has become the new love for the youth.

Ketamine is a liquid substance, which it can be converted into powder form after the evaporation. After the intake of Ketamine, it will block the sensational transmission of the chemical substance. It will create an empty feeling and develop near death hallucination. Even the person may have a strange headless hallucination toward the dancing partners.

It has been abused among youth because there is no legislation in the U.S.A. to regulate the use of Ketamine and there is no penalty in any states toward the Ketamine users. Overdose of Ketamine may cause death resulting from circulatory and respiratory failure.

How can parents prevent and reduce their adolescents' use of drugs:

Drug abuse has overwhelmingly become widespread in our society and our adolescents have more opportunity to obtain the illicit drugs than before. If infectious diseases can be prevented, then the temptation of drugs can be prevented also- as long as parents are willing to open their eyes and take steps to reduce the likelihood of their child's contact with drugs. Parents must also work to build the adolescent's confidence to reject them.

We can help them to develop the immunity to the drugs.

1. Set a good example and model behavior you want your adolescent to follow:

Children will learn what they got from parents. And what parents allow in moderation their children will do in excess. If the parents smoke, they will learn to smoke because they feel that smoking is rational. It is never too late for parents to quit smoking. Your giving up smoking is an announcement to the whole family that you are a responsible person. You are willing to hold you accountable to the family.

If you drink because of the social reasons, alleviating pain or reducing pressure or tension, this is indicative of telling your children "It is OK to drink". Unconsciously, children will recognize that drinking is permissible. For the sake of children, quitting drinking is worth the effort. If your relatives or other extended family members are drinking, you may tell your child that is not our business.

However, our family is an alcohol-free zone. Warn your adolescent that he or she may have a genetic predisposition toward alcoholism since those related to them are heavy drinkers.

If you have used illicit drugs regardless of the reason, you are proclaiming that you have approved of an illegal matter. Therefore, you have to get help before you ask your children say no to the drugs.

2. Establish the attitude and identity that are resistant to drugs use:

Adolescents seldom seek drugs to satisfy themselves, if they have experienced unconditional love from their parents. If we have learned together that our body is the temple of God, the Holy Spirit is living within. We cannot abuse our body even during our loneliness and we cannot try drugs because of our own curiosity.

We can help them to say no to drugs and help them to understand what is right or wrong and learn the consequence of drug use. It is advisable to encourage them to join the church youth group and related activities.

Once they have the sense of belonging, accepting the Lord and experiencing the everlasting love from Him, adolescents will have the cornerstone to build the solid foundation of their faith, which will prevent them from confrontation against God who loves them.

3. Begin early talk about smoking, alcohol, and drugs as opportunities arise:

We can begin the drug education from the age of 5 years. We may be starting to form the simple common knowledge and gradually getting into more detail and deeper. The education can be carried as opportunity for teaching.

For instance, if a famous person is dealing with the consequences of drug use (such as dropped out from a team or suffering legal consequences), make sure your adolescent hears the cautionary tale. If you hear that someone is smoking, drinking, inhaling, or injecting drugs, talk about it. What are they using? What consequences are likely? Why is it wrong? What help do they need?

In general, most 5th or 6th graders have the tendency of impulse to try drugs. If their parents are too overworked, over-committed, and overtired to keep tabs on the home front, the parents may wake up one day to find a major drug problem on the doorstep.

4. Do not allow your adolescent to go to a party, sleepover, or other activity that is not supervised by someone you trust:

Don't blindly believe that the presence of a grow-up guarantees a safe environment. Get to know your youth's friends' parents, not just his or her friends. Make certain that your child knows you will pick him or her up anytime, anywhere - no questions asked - if he or she finds himself /herself in a situation where drugs or alcohol are being used. And be sure to praise him or her for a wise and very mature decision if he or she does contact you.

5. Have the courage to curtail your adolescent's contact with drug users:

If you know that his friends are drug users, or actively use alcohol, you must impose restrictions on the relationship. You may stipulate that your adolescent can spend time with that person only in your home- without any closed doors and when you are around. If there is any sign that the drug-using friend is pulling your teenager toward his style, declare a quarantine right way.

By all means, if your teenager feels called to help a friend climb out of a drug problem, don't let him try it alone. Work as team to direct that person toward the recovery program. Otherwise, your teenager may be trapped instead of helping him up.

6. Create significant rules to discourage alcohol and drugs use:

Parents may make it very clear that you consider the use of cigarettes, alcohol, or illegal drugs a very serious matter. Judgment regarding punishments fitting crimes will be necessary. If your teenager confesses that he tried a cigarette or a beer at a party and expresses an appropriate resolve to avoid a repetition, heart-to-heart conversation and encouragement would be far more appropriate than summarily grounding him for six months.

If your teenager is warned repeatedly and still does not listen, you must establish and enforce some meaningful consequences. Loss of driving, dating, or even phone privileges for an extended period of time may be in order.

The teenager can easily avoid the penalty by staying clear of drugs and people who use them. If a friend starts to exert pressure to smoke, drink, or use drugs, he can say, "Sorry, I do not want to be stuck without transportation for the nest six months".

What to do if a problem has already developed.

1. Do not deny or ignore the problem.

Talk to your teenager about it. But also talk to siblings, friends, and anyone else who knows what he is up to. You may not like what you hear, but better to get the hard truth at present time than a ghastly surprise later. The marijuana cigarette you discovered may be a onetime experience or may be the tip of an iceberg.

2. Do not wallow in a false guilt:

Most of the parents feel a great deal of self-blame when a drug problem erupts at home. Parents may feel that they are not good parents to the teenager.

If you do carry some responsibility for what has happened, face up to it, confess it to God and your family, and then get on with the task of helping your teen.

Of course, your adolescent must deal with his or her own responsibility as well.

3. Seek help from persons who have the experience with treating drug problem:

Talk to your pastor and family physician because they can be part of your team even in a supporting role. If they are not able to help you completely, they may refer you to the professional who is experienced in organizing a family intervention. These may include educational sessions, individual and family counseling, medical treatment, and long-term follow-up. The goal is to convince the drug user in a firm but loving way of the need for change now.

The confrontation should include specific alternatives for the type of treatment he will undergo and a clear-cut "or else..." if he is not willing to cooperate.

If you need the help from the supporting association, you may contact the following for assistance:

(1) **Action of parent Support Program**
3959 Laurel Canyon Blvd., #L, Studio City, CA 91604
1-800- for- teen

(2) **Asian Pacific Family Center**
9353 E. Valley Blvd., Rosemead, CA 91770- 1934
(626) 287- 2988

For more information about drugs and their effects, prevention and treatments, call, read, or visit:

1-800-788-2800   **1-800-SINDROGAS**

www.TheAntiDrug.com or **www.health.org** or
www.NIDA.NIDA.NIH.gov
Growing Up Drug-free.
U.S. Department of Education.
Available by calling 1-877-433-7827

For a description of effective school and community prevention program and strategies, you can also visit http://modelprograms. samhsa.gov

4. Be prepared to make difficult "tough love" decisions:

If your drug-dependent teenager will not submit to treatment or will not give up his life style and insists on continuing the drug use, the parents will need to take a big step to inform him that he can not continue to live at home while carrying on this behavior. This decision will be necessary not only to motivate him to change but to prevent his drug- induced turbulence from destroying the rest of the family.

However, we have to present him with one or more options. These may include entering an inpatient drug-treatment center, halfway house, boot-camp program, or youth home, or staying with a relative or another family who is willing to accept him for a defined period of time. More possibilities may be discussed with him as making him a ward of the court or even turning him over to the police if he has been involved in criminal activity. If the parents continue to shield him from the consequences of his behavior or bail him out when his drugs get him into trouble, he will not change, and the parents will be left with deep-seated anger and frustration.

5. Do not expect a quick solution:

It may require intervention to make a drug problem go away. One conversation, counseling session, prayer time, or trip to the doctor won't be enough. You need a comprehensive response encompassing specific treatment and counseling for the gamut of your teen's life-home, school friends, and church.

6. The Bible reminds us of the father of the prodigal son (Luke 15: 11- 21):

The story of the father and his prodigal son indicates that "tough love" means allowing the consequences of bad decisions to be fully experienced by one who is making them. It also means that the parent loves the son so deeply and securely that it will never die. The Bible is suggesting never give up hope, never stop praying, and never slam the door on reconciliation and restoration when he comes to his senses.

16

Acne, Pimples, and Zits

Teenagers deal with numerous psychological and physiological issues during these formative years. For example, some teens emotionally struggle with feelings of inferiority. For many teens, acne is one of the most troublesome physical problems for teenagers. About 85% to 90% of teens develop some form of acne. The only difference is the individual severity. Therefore, you do not need to feel bad nor feel like you are the only one to suffer with acne. In reality, acne is a common problem among teens.

Generally speaking, girls tend to develop acne at an earlier age than boys. However, acne occurs in boys more frequently and with greater severity. While in most cases acne clears on it eventually, it should be treated and not ignored. The reason for this is that some of the physical and emotional scars it leaves can last many years.

There is no "cure" for acne. However, in order to treat it, we have to learn how acne develops. Acne occurs in the sebaceous follicles. These follicles are unlike hair follicles because they have large, abundant sebaceous glands and usually lack hair. The sebaceous glands (Figure 1) normally produce sebum, an oily substance that is secreted into the follicles. Sebaceous glands are largest and most fully developed on the face, scalp, upper chest, back and penis. Obstruction of the sebaceous follicle opening produces acne. If the obstruction occurs at the follicular mouth, it is called open comedone or a blackhead. If the obstruction is just beneath the follicular opening in the neck of the sebaceous follicle, it produces a visible bump commonly known as a pimple or whitehead.

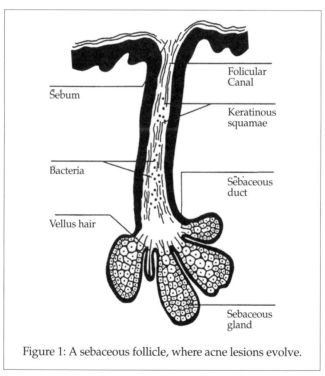

Figure 1: A sebaceous follicle, where acne lesions evolve.

The disorder has four primary pathogenic mechanisms: (1) follicular plugging, (2) bacterial colonization, (3) sebum overproduction, and (4) inflammation.

The illustrations are following:

(1) **Follicular plugging:** Acne develops when Keratinous squamae from the follicle wall plug the follicle canal. This abnormality in the keratin-forming process may be caused by hormonal stimulation of immature follicles. The plugging creates a micro comedone that may progress to form significant lesions as the blocked follicles dilate.

(2) **Bacterial colonization:** The follicular plugging permits the overgrowth of anaerobic organisms that reside deep in the follicle, such as Propionibaterium acnes ("P acnes"), Staphylococci Epdidermidis, Micrococci, and Pityrosporum.

(3) **Sebum overproduction:** In puberty, increased androgen production-Testosterone in men and adrenal dehydroepiandrosterone (DHEA) and ovarian testosterone in women- appears to stimulate sebaceous gland hyperplasia (overgrowth) and sebum production. The sebum overproduction may also contribute to bacterial overgrowth. The composition of the sebum is sequalene, wax esters, triglycedrides, and sterols.

(4) **Inflammation:** When "P acnes" and sebum are trapped in the blocked follicle, bacterial lipases break down triglycerides into free fatty acid, which promote inflammation. As a result of the immune responses to "P acnes" and formation of white blood cells in the follicle is disrupted. (Figure 2)

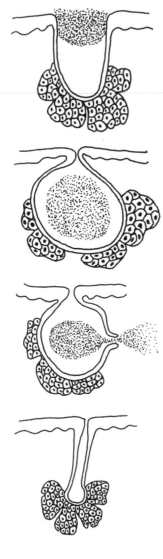

Open comedone; wide, patulous opening of sebaceous channel with plug of stratum corneum cells in follicular mouth.

Mircocomedone (closed comedone); obstruction of the follicular channel just beneath the opening.

Inflammatory papule; overgrowth of bacteria and rupture of the wall, producing a foreign body reaction surrounding the follicle.

Norman sebaceous follicles. Large sebaceous glands excrete sebum into cylindrical sebaceous channel.

Figure 2

Types of acne: Four types of acne lesions develop from microcomedones such as: (Figure 3)

1. **Black head, open comedones:** If the obstruction at the sebaceous follicle opening, a wide, patulous opening develops that is filled with a plug of slim stratum corneum cells. This is the formation of open comedone, or blackhead. The black color is caused not by dirt but oxidized melanin within the stratum corneum cellular plug. Open comedone is more common in early adolescence.

2. **White head, closed comedones:** An obstruction of the follicle just beneath the follicular opening in the neck of the sebaceous follicle produces a cystic swelling of the follicle duct. This is seen as microcomedones (closed comedone, or a whitehead). It is believed these microcomedones are the precursors of inflammatory acne. It is more common in children 8 to 10 years of age and in adolescents.

3. **Inflammatory comedones:** These lesions include firm, red papules, pustules, cysts, and rarely, interconnecting draining sinus tracts. Most adolescents have a mixture of micrcomedones, red papules, pustules, and blackheads.

4. **Cystic acne or nodular cystic comedone:** This type of acne requires prompt medical attention because a ruptured cyst or sinus tracts result in scar formation. Such a scar may return to normal skin color after several years. However, some adolescents have a tendency toward keloid formation especially over the sternal area (Figure 3)

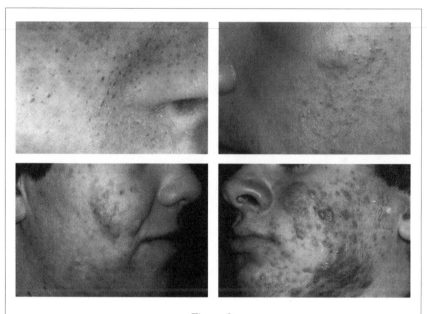

Figure 3

Acne is characterized by a variety of lesions. Typical patterns include open comedones (top left), open and closed comedones and papules (top right), papules, pustules, and nodules (bottom left), and numerous nodules (bottom right).

Treatment of acne:

There is no magic remedy, which will cure acne instantly. Do not believe the exaggerated advertisement of an instant cure. Time and patience are the best remedies. It is important to remember that treatment can only control acne, not cure it. Also keep in mind that once someone starts a treatment, it might be several weeks before a visible change is noticeable. For most of people, this problem will fade away before adulthood. Nonetheless, parents need to be empathetic and supportive of their teen during this time. Sometimes support will involve a gentle reminder to be consistent with treatment.

Medications commonly used for acne treatment include the following:

- **Benzoyl peroxide** kills the skin bacteria that cause inflammation and helps open the ducts through which sebum passes to the skin surface. It is available without a prescription in 2.5%, 5% and 10% in several forms. Liquids and creams are better for dry skin, while gel forms are more helpful for oily skin. Benzoyl peroxide can be applied once or twice daily after washing the affected area with mild soap and water. It will improve acne in the majority of cases if used consistently. This treatment helps to open pimples and unplug blackheads, and it also kills bacteria. An amount the size of a pea should cover most of the face. If the skin becomes red or peels, you are using too much or applying too often. So, slow down. This lotion may be needed for several years. If using benzoyl peroxide for one or two months does not help, a doctor should be consulted.

• **Tretinoin** (Avita or Retin-A in various forms and strength) is extremely effective in unplugging pores and even causing comedones (blackheads) to be expelled from the skin. This can be alarming at first because Tretinoin typically causes some redness and peeling of the skin. This effect is only temporary and it may last for 4-6 weeks. Skin treated with tretinoin sunburns more easily, so avoiding the sun or using a strong sunscreen is important. The combination of tretinoin applied at bedtime (thirty minutes after washing and drying the face) and benzoyl peroxide every morning should control 80% to 85% of acne in adolescents.

• **Antibiotics** applied topically or taken orally sometimes help by reducing the population of bacteria on the skin. An oral form of tetracycline or erythromycin is particularly helpful when inflammation is intense. However, pregnant women or children under 12 must not take tetracycline because these drugs discolor the teeth of a developing fetus or a child. Topical antibiotics are less effective than systematic antibiotics. 1% Clindamycin phosphate solution is the most efficacious topical antibiotic. 1.5% and 2% topical erythromycin solutions are effective; 1% topical tetracycline solution is minimally effective.

• **Isotretinoin** (Accutane), an extremely potent derivative of vitamin A, is used in the most severe cases of acne. Isotretinoin acts essentially like an enhanced version of tretinoin, and 90% of even the worst cases of acne will respond to treatment over a four-to-five month period. However, this drug has a number of potent side effects including dry skin, itching, and liver dysfunction. Therefore, the treatment should be under the supervision of dermatologist.

• **Azelaic acid** (Azelex) is a newer topical medication that is unrelated to the others listed above. It is derived from cereal grains and inhibits skin bacteria, decreases the sebum that blocks pores and reduces inflammation. It can be applied twice daily to skin that has just been washed and should be continued for four weeks before deciding whether or not it is helpful.

Guidelines for acne therapy

Types of acne	Treatment
Comedonal	Topical comedolytic and Topical antibiotics
Mild inflammatory	2% erythromycin, 5% benzoyl peroxide gel or combinations of topical antibacterials and comedolytic agent
Moderate inflammatory	Oral antibiotics and topical antibacterials, And comedolytic agents
Severe, scaring, or unresponsive	Isotretinoin administered under close guidance of a physician

Hints for teens to keep your acne under control

1. Keep your hands away from your face. Manipulation or squeezing blackheads and pimples can make them worse. It only ruptures intact lesions and provokes a localized inflammatory reaction.
2. Avoid picking or scratching pimples and pustules.
3. Avoid tight-fitting clothing or headgear, wet suits, helmets, headbands, and bras that rub skin may provoke changes in the skin are directly below them.
4. Keep your hair off your face. Cut, tie, or comb it as you please, but do not let it aggravate to your acne by spreading oil and bacteria.

5. Avoid oily soaps, moisturizing creams, oily hair preparations, and all heavy makeup. (Figure 4)

6. Oils and dyes in cosmetics and hair sprays can plug the sebaceous glands; so water-based products are better for people who are prone to acne. If you wear makeup, be sure to use water-base preparations.

7. Within the limits of a healthy diet, eat whatever you like. There is no evidence that diet affects acne. If you believe that you react to certain foods, keep a record of what happens each time you eat that particular food and eliminate that food if you are convinced that it causes your acne flares.

8. If tetracycline is prescribed, be sure to take it at least one hour before or two hours after mealtime. Never take milk, ice cream, or other dairy products within two hours before or after taking medicine. It is best to take medicine at bedtime with a glass of water. Other antibiotics can be taken with meals. Please ask for instructions.

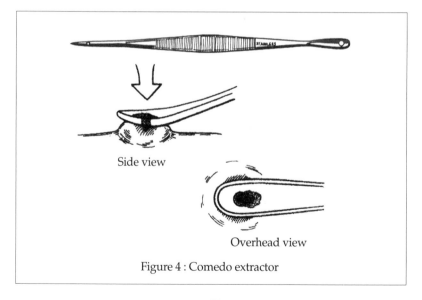

Side view

Overhead view

Figure 4 : Comedo extractor

9. Be patient. There is no quick or magic cure for acne, but following the treatment prescribed for you should bring real improvement after about two months.

10. Remember, treatment only controls acne; it does not cure it. Do not stop treatment because your skin clears up. Acne lesions begin at least a month before you can see them.

11. Learn to accept the ups and downs of acne activity. With persistence, you will ultimately see real improvement.

12. Some girls have a flare-up of acne before their menstrual periods. The reason for this is that it is in response to hormonal fluctuations when the outlet of the sebaceous gland becomes more obstructed.

13. Soap: Wash your skin twice each day- the most important time being at bedtime. Be sure to use a mild soap.

14. Hair: Keep your hair clean; consider washing it daily. Hair can make acne worse by its friction against the skin if it is too long.

15. Avoid picking: This keeps acne from healing.

16. Pimple opening: In general, it is better not to pop pimples. If you choose to do it anyway, do it safely. Never open a pimple before it has come to a head. Wash your face and hands first. Use a sterile needle (sterilized by alcohol or a flame). Nick the surface of the yellow pimple with the tip of the needle. The pus should run out without squeezing. Wipe away the pus and wash the area with soap and water. Scarring will not result from opening small pimples. However, it can result from squeezing boils or other large, red, tender lumps.

17. Blackheads that are a cosmetic problem can sometimes be removed with a blackhead extractor(Figure 4). This instrument costs about one dollar and is available at drugstores. By placing the hole in the end of the small metal spoon directly over the blackheads, uniform pressure can be applied that does not hurt normal skin. This method is much

more efficient than anything you can accomplish with your fingers.

Common Mistakes in Treating Acne:

1. Medicated soap, alcohol pad, and abrasive soap are not beneficial to the skin and will obstruct sebaceous glands outlets.
2. Avoid scrubbing the skin. Hard scrubbing is harmful to the skin, irritating sebaceous gland outlets and causing them to be shut tight.
3. Avoid applying oil-based cosmetics on facial skin. Doing so would obstruct sebaceous gland outlets. If necessary, consider using water-based cosmetics, but rinse thoroughly before sleep.
4. Avoid using moose or gel on hair, especially greasy hair tonics. With sweating, the mixture of these products and skin discharge would spread to face and chest, exacerbating acne.
5. Avoid applying friction and pressure on face and neck. For example, try not to wear bandanna, scarf, shawl, and necktie or turtleneck sweater. Do not rest your face and neck on your hand either. All these could aggravate acne.
6. Avoid shaving facial hair too close to the skin just to have a good impression for your date. Doing so will often scrape open sebaceous gland outlets and exacerbate acne.
7. Avoid taking high-dose zinc or vitamin A without doctor's direction. High-dose zinc might cause stroke, and high-dose vitamin A might cause brain swelling or bone pain.

Course of Acne:

Acne usually lasts until 20 or 25 years of age. It is rare for acne to leave any scars, and people worry needlessly about this if they treat acne with due care.

17

Choice of School

Most adolescents will discover that in junior high school, teachers tend to cover all aspect of teaching—they spend more time explaining, analyzing, supervising, and helping with your schoolwork. Teachers of senior high school like to give more challenging assignments—allowing students to learn on their own and develop thinking ability. In high school, students need to spend more time researching. In college and university, the academic atmosphere intensifies but you also have more freedom to pursue your interests. In order to learn something, you must have the self-discipline to work hard on your own. Professors only open the windows for you; you have to search for the knowledge.

In American high schools, teachers often train students to think independently. Students are trained to think logistically reasoning and be creative.

They are encouraged to be well-rounded persons—not only achieving academic excellence, but also excelling in sports and leadership. A teacher's goal is not just to train a mere scholar, but a leader who has good interpersonal skill and who will be a strong leader in society one day. Many parents from Asia wrongfully think that as long as their children excel in school, it is good enough; other extra curricular activities are unimportant. Consequently, many students with outstanding grades fail to get into good universities or colleges because most schools are looking for students with good grades and potential leadership quality. They want to have students who have had extra curricular activities, show leadership quality, and strong interpersonal skills. They also weight recommendation letters from teachers and counselors. From recommendation letters, universities and colleges try to understand prospective students' character, personality and interests. College admission standards usually consist of forty percent (40%) SAT score and cumulative grade average, twenty percent (20%) recommendation letters and interview. At this juncture I want to alert parents to encourage your adolescents to keep good grades but also to be active in extra curricular activities as well as church activities. Give them every opportunity to gain knowledge, leadership and interpersonal skills.

Forty percent (40%) to sixty percent (60%) of American high school graduates consider continuing education beyond high school. Many Asian parents are prejudiced about colleges and universities. Parents often insist that their adolescent's select famous universities only. They would not consider lesser-known colleges; actually this concept is wrong and not very practical in the United States.

Higher education institutes can be roughly divided into three groups:

1. University

A university is made up of at least three colleges. It offers a broad range of both undergraduate and graduate degree programs and is grouped into two categories, private and public. In general, a university has a big student body, huge campus, and is well known. Some private universities are better known than public universities, such as Harvard University, Stanford University, and Duke University, etc. Some public universities are also very famous, such as University of California — Berkeley and University of California — Los Angeles, etc. At these universities, there are undergraduate schools, which grant bachelor's degrees and graduate schools, which grant Master's and Doctoral degrees.

A university is known by its unique reputation of research. The freshman and sophomore classes at university are usually huge, ranging from 100 to 200 students in one classroom. Most of the teaching and guiding are done by teaching-assistants. Professors have little contacts with students. Therefore to write a recommendation letter professors can only reply on grades, unless they know you personally. A curve grading method is usually used in university — approximately only ten to fifteen per cent of students get A's, the rest get B's and C's. In general it is a good idea for self-motivated and intelligent high school graduates to go to university to receive education.

However, most of the professors at a university prefer research and writing.

Unconsciously they will pay more attention to graduates students because these students can enhance the professors research projects as well as improve the university's and the professor's reputation.

2. Liberal Arts College

A liberal arts college is intended to provide chiefly general knowledge and to develop the general intellectual capacities. Curriculum consists of liberal arts and sciences, which is grouped into the natural sciences, social sciences, and humanities. Classes are usually small (20 to 50 students) and grades are normally given in actual numbers. Professor's primary job is teaching, secondary being research. Therefore, professors can spend more time in contact with students and students can get more meaningful recommendation letters.

Liberal arts colleges emphasize human relations. Graduates from these colleges can easily get into other universities for advanced degrees, such as master's and doctoral degrees, or professional schools like law and medical schools. Most of liberal colleges only offer master's degrees. A few also offer doctoral degrees. Most of the liberal arts colleges are private with high tuition. There are many famous liberal arts colleges, such as Elmhurst College, Pomona College, Swarthmore College, William & Mary College, etc. Admission standards of these colleges are as high as the most famous universities. It is an excellent choice for those students who like a small school environment and also wish to learn interpersonal skills as well as have more attention.

3. Community college

The community colleges are set up for social districts. They offer two years of education beyond high school with low tuition to help lower income students or people who want to go to college after having worked a job. Many high school graduates enter community colleges to get associate degrees or equivalents. Then they transfer to a four-year college or university as a junior. Due to keen competition in the universities, ten percent (10%) of students drop out during freshman and sophomore years. Therefore, there is room to accept transferring community college graduate or other college students.

If you have difficulty deciding on a university or college, consider your interest, aptitude, and subjects of interest. If you cannot decide before high school graduation, you need to seek the help of school counselors. They will probably advise you not to go to a difficulty university if you have to work hard to get good grades. Most students in a better-known university are cream of the crop.

If you compete with them, you might lose your self-confidence. It is better to go to an easier school where you have a better chance to get good grades. Having good grades will get you into a graduate school. On the contrary, college graduates with mediocre grades from a more competitive university will have trouble getting into a better graduate school. By then it is too late to regret. Small college graduates who have good foundation, good grades and good recommendation letters will easily get into better graduate schools. American graduate schools like to admit students from other universities and send their graduates to other universities in order to achieve academic exchange.

If you plan to attain a bachelor's degree, I would advise you to select the best school.

If you plan to get a master's or a doctoral degree, select the most suitable undergraduate school and then select the best graduate school for advanced degree. Most employers only look at your last degree when hiring. Therefore, your last degree is the most important.

Per chance, you cannot go to a university for a while. Do not feel bad. Many people re-enter college after having entered the job market. These people usually value education more and are more dedicated to studying. They end up getting excellent grades. If you have no chance to go to a college or university at all, you need not feel discouraged, either. Man's success does not depend on formal education alone. One of the success factors is continual learning, which you can do and is in your control.

Some students who graduate in the top percentile of a class fail to perform as well as their classmates in lower percentile because of, according to some research, ego, superiority complex, and poor interpersonal skills. At work, they act isolated, self-admired, and uncooperative with coworkers. Therefore, if you are a top-notch student, thank God for your intelligence, talent, and opportunity. Ask Him to help you become humble, cooperative, and friendly. Success does not depend on intelligence quotient (IQ) alone; it also depends on emotional quotient (EQ) and interpersonal skill.

In Taiwan, high school graduates must take an entrance examination to go to college or university. The result of that examination determines a student's admission. Further, those results are used to match the student's selection of majors. Some students fill out the application form according to subjects of interest. Other students only consider the reputation of a university or college. For the students who only consider the reputation of the school, they may be admitted into a department of their disliking.

In these instances, some transfer into a department of their interest after beginning their studies in higher education. Others yet retake the college entrance exam while in undergraduate studies. Once admitted into a department of their liking, their studies start over entirely. Keeping these things in mind, it is important to consider your interest, social trend, and demand of professional field when making your choice. Consequently, the experience of your parents, family members, and friends can be valuable reference to you.

Taiwan is changing its policy with regard to college admissions. Specifically, new Taiwanese high school graduates who are seeking college education are faced with the American College System. Colleges and universities are looking not only at test results but the overall performance of the student while in high school. In addition, undergraduate schools emphasize the importance of English comprehension and reading abilities. Graduate schools in Taiwan not only emphasize these English skills but also actually mandate it.

Some Taiwanese high school graduates wish to complete their undergraduate studies in the United States. For some, this is a good idea. In order to do so, however, a good grade points average and a good score in the TOEFL (Test of English as foreign language) examination is beneficial for undergraduates. For those applying to graduate schools, the GRE (Graduate Record Examinations) is also required in addition to the TOEFL. Some universities reserve admission quotas specifically for foreign students. The schools reserve these admissions in an attempt have a solid exchange of international scholars. Whether you apply for admission to a university, liberal arts college, or community college, one of the most important prerequisite is to have a good proficiency in English. Having a good command of the English language will serve you well during both the admission process and your actual studies.

18

The State of Immigrant Families

1. The Emotional State

When the Chinese people migrated to America, whether they were from Taiwan, Mainland China, Hong Kong or Southeast Asia, they encountered a totally new environment. When faced with a diverse culture, a new language and a different way of living, they usually experience a culture shock and have a difficult time adjusting to the new way of life. In the Asian culture, people like to "save face" and usually pretend that everything is going smoothly. However, they do not have peace in their hearts and they have constant struggles. It is very difficult for them to express their pain and suffering to others, especially in dealing with their own teenage children.

People migrated to America for many reasons. Some people just migrated without a clear understanding of why they were moving.

This type of people usually has the hardest time in settling into the new environment. After they migrate and face the reality that their dream and the reality are utterly different, it becomes very difficult for them to accept and they will encounter more and more problems. This situation usually happens to people who used to live very comfortably in their homeland and now they have to start all over from scratch in America. Encountered with a different environment filled with different culture, language, habit and ways of living, the pressure mounts for them to simply survive. The pressure would increase even more when they have communication and relationship problems with their children who are becoming "Americanized".

2. The Difference of Family Values between the East and the West

(1). Addressing of the Elders

East: Chinese respect the elders. They usually believe the elders have more experience and capabilities. When people encounter difficult situations, they will seek advice from the elders. They show respect and order by calling an elder uncle whether he is a relative or not. The elders usually have authority and are well respected.

West: People usually call others by first name to show familiarity or closeness. The first generations of immigrant parents are not used to this manner. They generally believe this manner shows disrespect and is inferior to the Asian culture.

Recommendation: Have an open mind. Try to understand the

cultural difference between the East and the West.

(2). The Attitude to Children

East: After immigration, the Chinese parents set high expectations for their children. In order to achieve these expectations, they are willing to do anything to send their children to all the best and "most famous" schools. They spend all of their time and effort to grasp any opportunity that will make their kids successful. They become full-time drivers for the kids and take the kids to different school activities, competitions, art classes, Chinese school, music lessons and tutoring classes. As a result, the parent sacrifices their own time, money and plans but the kids may not show any appreciation toward them.

The kids instead may feel there is enormous pressure that they are not able to breathe. This effort usually results in conflict.

West: The parents do not pay as much attention to goals and plans for kids and do not force the kids as such. They respect individuality and let the kids explore their own talents.

Solution: Chinese parents should set a limit. The parents are not super human and do get tired. The parents should have their own space and teach the kids to have mutual respect and support. The respect and support should be bi-directional. If the respect and support only goes from parents to kids, the kids will command authority and the parents will only suffer.

(3). Expression of Emotion

East: When parents go through stages of sadness, emotional turmoil or anxiety, they seldom express their feelings. They rarely express any emotion toward the children whether they are on good or bad behavior and thus the kids do not know how to behave. Furthermore, the parents believe that it is the kids' duty to overachieve. They do not praise kids nor show any feelings of pride for their accomplishments. However, they usually scold and embarrass the kids in front of other people when the kids are not behaving. When parents are communicating with the kids, they are usually more reserved and conservative and thus cause miscommunication or no communication between family members.

Chinese generally do not express their opinions openly in front of others or in meetings, especially when they are in disagreement. After an agreement is reached, they will either privately or semi-privately express their discontent. The Chinese have the tendency to avoid confrontations but expect others to understand.

West: The westerners express their emotions strongly and clearly articulate their feelings. This is usually very difficult for immigrants to accept. When teenagers come back from school and openly express their thoughts and opinions, it is difficult for parents to accept such outbursts.

In meetings, westerners would express their thoughts and opinions openly, try to influence opinions, and reach consensus. In the midst of discussions, there might be strong arguments. However, once a consensus is reached, everyone will put aside the differences and try to perform together to achieve the goal. They do not expect others to readdress their concerns.

Solution: Learn to communicate. Try to have mutual understanding and support, and learn to compromise. Learn to express opinions openly and let others understand your issues and concerns. Learn to find consensus through communication. Do not use authority or pressuring tactics to suppress others. It is best to use equal status to communicate with others.

(4). Family Values and Traditions

East: Elders usually use a tone of seniority to teach kids. They believe that it is best for the elders to have the final say; otherwise things are likely to fail.

The elders will usually treat each family member's success or achievement as the family's success and achievement. The parents treat the family as a unit and usually set everyone's goals as the family's goal. If the children do not follow the family's goal, they will likely anger the parents and suffer repercussions.

West: Westerners respect individual freedom. People decide for themselves and seldom ask elders for advice. The person's success or failure does not necessary reflect the family's success or failure. Westerner does not have to meet parent's goals and satisfy parent's expectations.

Solution: Use communication to understand the cultural differences and use the difference to bridge the gap in understanding.

Do not force the children to satisfy the family's expectations and do not pressure them to adapt.

3. Characteristics of Immigrants

(1). Immigrants are Less Open at Social Events

Influenced by two different cultures, immigrants are very conscious of comparisons of character and they care a great deal of what others think of them. Therefore, immigrants are usually very nervous and they are more difficult to cooperate with others. They are also more afraid of taking responsibilities so they would not result in failure.

When teenagers bring friends home from school, the immigrant parents do not usually have direct communication with the friends. In school events or parent-teacher conferences, the immigrant parents are usually by themselves.

(2). Immigrants are less likely to Express Opinions

Immigrants are less likely to express their opinions and state their intentions. Nevertheless, the teenagers are taught to express thoughts and opinions openly by the teachers in school.

Parents sometimes are very stubborn and will not compromise. The immigrant parents are usually more introverted and they expect others or teenagers to understand their feelings. However, during meetings or discussions, they are not willing to share their true intentions. When decision does not meet what they wanted, they usually complain afterwards.

(3). Second-Generation Boys are more Introverted

Influenced by their immigrant parents, second-generation boys are usually more introverted and are unwilling to share their opinions. Some boys are influenced by Asian traditions and believe that men are more superior. As a result, second-generation girls are not willing to date with second-generation boys. They are more likely going to befriend with American boys who are more open, caring, active and willing to share their true feelings. They also respect women more than the second-generation boys.

A research study has found that fifty percent(50%) of second-generation Japanese girls marry Americans and seventy percent(70%) of third-generation girls marry Americans.

(4). Strong Belief in Sex Difference

Asian males are more likely to be male-chauvinistic. It is more difficult for them to accept equal partnership between the sexes. This is simply an Asian tradition. On the other hand, American boys always say "ladies first" and let girls have their way. However, after marriage, Asian males usually give up financial control, open joint accounts and let wives take over the finances.

American boys generally believe in separate bank accounts and makes clear on whom should pay for expenses of the household. This behavior, which is a world apart from the dating period, may be one of the major reasons of divorce between American husbands and their Asian wives.

(5). Chinese are more Serious in American Society

Immigrant parents are usually more serious and conservative. They rarely get into the mainstream of American lifestyle. They often pay attention to their own surroundings and do not care as much about others. The language barrier and the lack of social opportunities with westerners may have caused this attitude.

(6). Identity Crisis

New immigrants face a crisis in their own identities. Sometimes they feel like outcasts that are neither Asians nor Americans. They want to understand and absorb the American culture yet they cannot let go of the their own culture. This causes confusion for the teenager children. The children learn western culture in school and society and yet have to adapt to Chinese culture at home. This has been a point of contention in new immigrant families. The best way to resolve the contention is to let the teenagers understand where they came from and have the parents adapt an attitude that they are willing to change and accept western culture.

Sometimes parents like to demote themselves and thus hurt the children's self-confidence. The parents have to train the kids to treat the two cultures as equals and let them experience both cultures by encouraging them to go to social activities or short-term missions. Parents should take a global view and work on their language, communication and social skills.

Parents should also take courage and speak in front of others and not be afraid of accents. In truth, accents can only be eliminated before a person reaches sixteen since the structure of the inner ear and mouth can still adapt and accept new language. But after sixteen, the accents will be difficult to eliminate because the structure of the inner ear is slower to adapt and the oral structure is not as flexible. The new immigrants should not be self-conscious about their accents. Most Americans are very willing to listen no matter what the accents are. As long as you demonstrate your ability and have good relationship with others, the society is willing to accept us. Sometimes accents can even be used as an advantage!

(7). Narrower Social Adaptation

Because of the difference in eastern and western culture, the ways of measuring what is socially acceptable are also different. Therefore, new immigrants should not adhere to the old standards or just chase to adapt new western standards. This is especially true in couple relationships. The husband works and experiences more of the western culture while the wife stays home and does not have the chance to experience the culture. The wife then would feel more constraint at home and be very demanding on everything the husband does.

Couple relationships could be further strained on difference in perspectives and thus people grow apart. The couple would then start to argue on little things or principles. Similarly, parents and teenagers would also grew apart or argue because of difference in principles, perspectives or family values.

(8). Lack of Political Activities

Because of political suppression in both Taiwan and China in previous generations, most immigrants would just settle for a peaceful life without political involvement. This attitude of avoiding politics at all cost is very apparent in first-generation immigrants. However, the United States is a free country. People are involved in politics through elections and utilize political channels to achieve their goals. First-generation immigrants usually pay more attention to their work instead of their political rights and thus lose many changes to vote or run for election.

The solution is to understand and join the American political system and not give up the rights to vote or take part in political opportunities. Use votes to express opinions and encourage kids to study law and political science. With the parents' active involvement, the kids would one day have a voice in political systems or social groups and be the salt and light for the Lord.

(9). Difference between Expectation and Reality

Immigrant parents often hope the teenage children would excel at music and the Chinese language. However, when the children choose music or humanities as their occupational study, parents are almost always against the choice. The parents believe that there is no future in studying music or humanities and so they would limit the children's rights to choose. Parents' reason that there is a better future by studying engineering, science, law or medicine and they are afraid that the children cannot support themselves. In reality, there are much more opportunities for the children than the first-generation parents, and their language skills and social adaptation are much better than the parents. More career choices are available in America and should be considered if the teenage wishes to pursue.

Another problem is the parents only encourage the children to study and get the best grades in class, but we seldom encourages them to participate in sports, competitions or other social activities. As a result, the best universities reject many good students because they do not have experiences in leadership or discipline training. The way to resolve this situation is to look at how the American universities evaluate the students. The schools are looking for students that have diverse skills in academics, leadership and teamwork because these skills will assist the students to become leaders of tomorrow.

In a typical American family, parents are usually not as involved in financial planning for paying the tuition. They will only make suggestions to students and encourage them to borrow loans for their college and pay them back after they graduate. Chinese parents will save all they can to pay for the children's tuition but sometimes they would intrude on the children's right of privacy and decision-making. When children do not follow the parents' advice, the parent will create pressure or even confrontation that destroys their relationship.

In everyday lives, we have to keep learning to grow in God's love to accept and cooperate with one another, encourage each other with God's Word and communicate honestly and openly. This is the way to resolve conflicts and confrontations.

The Classification of problems faced by Immigrants

If teenagers can understand the problems faced by their immigrant parents, they may understand and sympathize what their parents are going through.

(1). Language Barrier at Work

Western employers usually stereotype immigrants. On one hand they want the immigrants to work hard. On the other hand the employers do not want the immigrant employees to complain or raise issues. The first-generation immigrants mostly fit into this stereotype. In research labs and companies, most Eastern immigrants perform well in their jobs. However, because of language barriers and lack of communication skills, they do not often express their thoughts or participate in discussions. Consequently, some people will not treat them with respect and so they are slow to receive promotions since they are perceived as not having leadership potential. Even though the immigrants may be unhappy about the situation, they generally feel helpless and some even believe it is a type of racism.

In truth, because we do not express opinions, the boss does not know what we are capable of without long and careful observation. If we can improve our language and communication skills, eliminate the thought that we are inferior to others, maintain good relationship with bosses and colleagues, grasp opportunities to build understanding and take management courses, we should be able to break the "glass ceiling" mentality. We can also utilize the skills to get into politics.

(2). Lack of Belief in Equal Opportunity

Many societies in the East are male dominated; however, the western societies try to achieve equal opportunity for both sexes. Chinese employers are generally not used to expressing gratitude, and employees often feel unappreciated. For example, if we do not send a birthday card or celebrate special events for employees, the employees would mostly likely feel the employer is stingy and unapproachable. We should learn to adapt the habits.

If we celebrate for the teenagers in family gathering or birthday parties, this will encourage the teenagers mentally, improve communications, and draw the family closer as a unit.

(3). Negligence to the need of the Elders

Parents of new immigrants or grandparents of the teenagers often feel neglected and as burden to their children because they are old and cannot adapt to the new environment. They are caged in their homes: they are blind since they do not read English; they are deaf because they do not understand English and they are crippled because they cannot drive. Every time they would like to go out, they have to wait for their kids to come back home. However, they usually are afraid to ask since the children has been working all day and they are tired. Sometimes they speak up, then an argument would ensue accusing them of not caring about how others feel or they are spoiling the grand kids. The tension then builds after each argument and eventually each side would accuse each other and destroy their relationship.

There are senior communities, senior groups and senior

counseling in America to focus on the issue of senior citizens in society. Some are specifically geared to help Asian seniors here in Southern California. After year 2000, senior citizens would represent twenty-five to thirty percent (25-30%) of the whole population. Senior citizens usually suffer from depression and are sometimes suicidal. If you are living in a large family with grandparents, parents and kids, the issues about senior citizens has to be recognized and paid close attention to avoid confrontations.

(4). Isolation from Society

Some immigrant families keep minimum contacts with the outside world. After a while, the family members would start developing psychological problems and physical diseases that may worsen and develop into stomach problems, emotional distress, sleep disorder, among others. Some teenagers may develop drug habits, psychopathic diseases or even suicidal behavior.

The more isolated the family is from the outside, the easier to become an extremist or to develop strange behaviors. If the family isolates itself and does not participate in social gatherings or group events such as Sunday worship or church fellowship, it is very prone to develop problems. It is recommended for families to get involved in church groups, sport groups and other social organizations.

(5). Drug Habits

Asians rarely developed drug habits in the past. However, studies have shown that more and more Asian teenagers are using drugs today. Everyone is looking for happiness. If they cannot find happiness, they might start to use alcohol or drugs to find happiness or to get high. This is a desperate attempt to find happiness that does not exist in the real world. However, once they develop the habit, it is very difficult to move away from it.

Most people who have religious beliefs are not drug users. This is because they utilize prayer, Bible study and religious beliefs to ask God for help. His mercy and guidance will give the believers peace, joy and power to face the problems.

(6). Strong Depression

There are two different kinds of depression: uni-polar anxiety and multi-polar anxiety. People suffering from multi-polar anxiety usually are suicidal. When grownups come to America, most of their characteristics have been developed and therefore they are less affected by culture shock and suffer less anxiety. The people who suffer the most from anxiety are around twenty years old since they face the most problem in adapting to the new environment and adjusting between the old and new culture. They are likely to be anxious and experience symptoms such as sadness, desperation, whining, fear, and slowness to perform.

Furthermore, some teenagers might demonstrate antisocial tendencies, strange behaviors, lying, stealing, and running away from home or psychopathic symptoms.

(7). Self-pity

Because they are not fluent in English, first-generation immigrants tend to have a feeling of self-pity. This feeling transfers to the children and the children will look down on their original culture and family values. Self-pity and anxiety are closely linked.

The way to solve self-pity in children is not to "educate" children to understand Chinese culture, but to let them have opportunities to "experience" culture. Let them join activities that are related to Chinese culture and they will adapt and accept both Chinese and American culture.

(8). Inability to Deal with New Relationships

Immigrants were already affected by their original culture. Once migrated, they have to face the impact of the new culture and new ways of things. Because they may lack the experience to deal with people in the new environment, it is difficult for immigrants to build relationships. When the immigrants have difficulties in relationships, they are likely to show symptoms of emotional distress.

For example, some will suffer from asthma or chest pain when they are extremely nervous. Some immigrants even show temporary amnesia after they have a fight with bosses. They are likely to suspect and accuse relatives, friends or coworkers because they do not understand what was being said. Some immigrants would question the abilities of physicians.

(9). Inability to Adapt to New Social Manners

The Chinese do not usually make appointments to see doctors and they like to feel they have privileges. When they are searching for doctors or lawyers, they prefer that others make special referrals and use special privileges to finish matters. They especially do not trust doctors from other races. When Chinese come to see doctors, they expect a shot. If a doctor only gives them a prescription, they generally feel it is not enough. The patients also expect to be treated quickly. Most Chinese patients would not participate in group therapy. They prefer one-to-one treatment.

In public forums, the Chinese usually want to hear what other has to say but does not want to share their thoughts and opinions. This behavior does not work in the Western society.

The Chinese people like to come visiting friends unexpectedly. They do not call the host first, they just invite themselves to the friend's house. This is viewed as intruding on personal privacy in American society and is not welcomed even though it is very popular in Chinese society. Because of cultural differences, each country's social manner is also different and immigrants should respect the country's socially acceptable manners and traditions.

(10). Inability to Trust Other People's Suggestions

Many new immigrants do not understand how things work or what is socially acceptable in the US. They do ask friends or relatives for their opinions. However, they often do not adapt the opinions but rather ask around for more opinions before they decide what to do. This is especially apparent when they come to see doctors. They will initially follow the doctor's orders. However, after their condition improves, they will go against the doctor's advice and stop using the medicine. The best example is in using antibiotics, which requires them to take the medicine for seven to ten days in general. The patient usually stops around three days to save the medicine for the next time they are sick. Some even take the medicine and give them to friends or relatives. This attitude of not respecting expert opinions sometimes costs the patient to suffer severe consequences. This habit is very rampant in Asian countries and the immigrants generally do not correct it after they come to the America. Immigrants must change these habits for their own health and the health of their families.

In talking to friends and relatives, many immigrants will discuss their health problems. Sometimes people will use their own experience and opinions to give medical advice. This will slow down the time to get the right treatment. In American society, most people will not treat personal opinions as expert advice and would instead refer health issues to doctors.

When immigrant parents spend time with their children, the children usually will bring back some information about the new environment, especially on fashion. If parents are strict on tradition and are not willing to accept new thinking, this behavior will only bring embarrassment to the children in front of their friends. These events will cause the teenagers to look down on the parents and always disagree with them. It is better to listen to the children and learn from them and their friends. Your children will have more respect for you if they feel you listen to them and care about their fears, worries and opinions.

19

Advice to adolescents

Adolescence is a period of growth in youth. It is the most difficult period of one's life journey caused by growth spurt and unpredictable mood changes. This is a period of confusion and spiritual void. Before reaching full maturity, an adolescent is anxious to absorb all kinds of knowledge and experience. Thus, he/she is very susceptible to influences by friends and environment. But remember that though friends' opinions are important and affect you deeply, your friends are also in the searching and changeable period of life. Therefore, you need guidance from your parents, older siblings, pastor and counselor. Aversion to authority is one of the natural instincts of the adolescent. Often, you do not know what you are doing. Deep down you do care about our parents' suggestions and when there is an important decision to make, you will go along with parents.

But on the surface, it appears just the opposite- you show resistance to parental guidance. No wonder your parents are very baffled by your behavior!

All adolescents desire to have friends of the opposite sex. You all want to fall in love. But the spark of love is very short. It is like a flower. When the sun is too strong, the flower will wither. Love fades whenever there is a fight.

Please remember, thirty years from now you are likely to become the parent of an adolescent. Though you have vowed not to make the same mistakes as your parents, your adolescent will probably say that you are "old fashioned," because you will look at things differently from how you view things today. Now you may say to your parents, "You don't know anything!" One day your children will be like you today and say to you, "You don't know anything!"

I have seen some youths who go off the right path during adolescence and continue many of their behaviors when they become adults. They embarrass family members and friends. They themselves feel uneasy in social function. I have also seen many adolescents who have gone to colleges and universities and return home completely changed. They dress neatly and have good manners. As they mature, they develop very different view on life. They are like worms emerging from cocoons to become beautiful butterflies.

Adolescents are inclined to think that "now is forever." They think that present condition will never change and it will last for a lifetime. For instance: if he/she is not well-accepted and loved during adolescence, he/she thinks it will be the same for the rest of his/her life. Actually, it is not like that at all. Adolescence is a fleeting period. It will only leave you with some vague memories. Friends in your class will head off different directions after graduation. Today's scene will not be repeated. Your social groups in the elementary school, junior and senior high schools will be like clouds in the sky- same patterns will not appear twice.

You are now faced with a confusing, crazy, and upside down world. There are so many demands and challenges — romances end up like the Battle of Waterloo, defeated and rejected; no invitation to the important party; parents forever unsatisfied with whatever you do; acne, pimples, and zits keep on attacking you on the forehead, face, chest and back; you wonder if God really exists and cares about you. You want to give up because of all these painful experiences. But please remember this, "Everything will be normal again!"

An adolescent is like a bamboo shoot emerging from the ground. After thunderstorms and heavy wind, it becomes a sturdy green piece of bamboo. Adolescence is also like a tunnel — you go in and you come out. If you hold on to your steering-wheel firmly and pay close attention to direction, you will come out of the tunnel safely. The conflict, anxiety, and helplessness during adolescence will all disappear with time. There is a brand new world waiting for you!

You will face many temptations and worries. Some friends will use every possible means to get you to conform with them, to the extent of forcing you to do things you do not want to do, such as drinking, smoking tobacco and marijuana, and using illicit drugs, etc. You feel uncomfortable about all these things. Yet, you are afraid of losing their friendship so you feel tempted to go along.

However, experiences have taught us a very valuable lessons: If you stick to your principles and dare to be different by engaging God's given courage and strength and sincerely telling your friends your promise to God, you will be respected. Not only will they not sever your friendship, they will also respect you and admire your determination and courage. In case some of them still insist on forcing their ways on you, you might as well give up those friends who disregard your decision. Look for new friends who trust you and respect you. The reason adolescent's pressure their friends to conform are the fear of being betrayed. Since adolescence in only a passing phase of life, you can ask Jesus to help you get through this period. One day when you look back, you will discover the power faith has given you. When you grow up, you will know that adult friends will not force you to make decisions. Instead, adult friends will respect all your decisions.

What would you do if you do not have a good relationship with your parents?

Do you remember when you were just born? You depended on your parents one hundred percent for a long period of time. You could not do anything. Every need depended on your parent. Little by little you learned to do things for yourself and your parents also handed over some responsibility to you. They gave you help when you had some difficult and complicated problems. Under your parent's guidance, you have gradually learned to be independent.

Youths first taste independence around 13 or 14. Progressively they want to get away from parental control. They want to decide everything for themselves and live their own lives. They are annoyed by any parental disciplines. They are anxious to prove that they are no long little children. However, parents know their adolescents are not fully independent and they still need to give guidance on certain areas.

The interesting truth is that while adolescents are eager to escape parental control, they still depend on their parents. In other words, adolescents want freedom but not responsibility. That is not possible. Adolescents want free meals, free lodging, and tuition and medical bills paid. But they do not want parents to express any opinion. If a person is not self-sufficient, he does not deserve to have total freedom. Your family is not unique — there are tens of million families around the world fighting this 'freedom' problem. If you and your parents are currently having conflicts, it is only temporary. It is a phase of growth progress. It does not mean that you do not love your parents or your parents do not love you. It only means that your demand of freedom is beyond the limit permitted by your parents.

Whenever conflicts occur, it is best to openly discuss the subject to express and exchange opinions. If the freedom your parents give you is not reasonable, tell them that you have grown up and you should have the privilege to decide for yourself and take on more responsibility. Please remember that your demand must be reasonable. Throwing temper tantrums does not help the matter. It only makes people think you are irrational and immature. If your parents insist on their opinion, I suggest you obey them. After all they care about you more than anybody else in the world. No parents ever mean to do bad things to their beloved children.

I would like to publish a letter from a parent who tells us the stand he took regarding his adolescent's demand for freedom.

First of all, I as a parent hope you will know my deep love for you.

To be your parent, to raise you, and to watch you grow is the most precious privilege God has given me. I know you have entered adolescence and you want more freedom. I understand you want to be independent; you want to decide everything for yourself. However, I do not think you have the ability to use your independence responsibly. Therefore, we often clash. I only hope that we will not become enemies.

You know I will give in whenever possible. I respect your opinion. I try to understand you and your feelings. I am not a dictator who disregards your needs and desires. I love you and I want to make you as happy as possible.

I know my judgment will lead to unhappy conflict. Nonetheless, I dare myself to refuse your demands, thus causing tension and friction between us. I just want you to remember that you are my most beloved. And you love me, too. I hope we can be united to overcome this eminent obstacle and differences. I would not do that for another. I do this to you only because you are my child. I am willing to risk making you angry to express my opinion. If a person loses his family's support, this world will be a cruel place. Therefore, every family member must cling to our mutual love and care. When you grow up, you will look at these conflicts and fully understand my deep love for you. Until your wings are fully grown I will not let you fly with your total freedom. You will be grateful for what I have done. I want to thank you now for your patience. I also thank God for giving me this experience. Let's grow up together.

You must remember that you have a friend, who created you, understands you, and cares about you. When you are happy, He shares your happiness. When you cry, He shares your sorrow. When you face important choices (school, profession, or mate) He will guide your steps. Proverbs 3:6 say, "In all your ways acknowledge Him, and He will make your paths straight. " What a comforting promise! Are you willing to extend your hand to let Him guide you through your life's journey?

Please allow me to tell you a very touching story. Thirty years ago, I met an active, lovely young lady. She was born in Hong Kong. When she was eight, she got a strange disease called 'Lupus Erythematosus.' This is an illness caused by autoimmune disorder. In autoimmune disorder, the body produces antibodies against its own cells. Her parents sought many doctors to cure her but her illness did not improve at all. Then the whole family moved to New York City with the hope of finding a better doctor. Her parents hired the best doctor in town. But it was a disease without cure at that time. Her joints and skin were affected. Her skin rashes would get worse whenever exposed in the sun. Years of treatments with Steroid and Immunosuppressive drugs did not bring any improvement. She just got worse. Her heart, kidney, and brain all were invaded by the disease. Finally, she died and went to heaven; her parents were very sad.

Because this patient was a rare case, the doctor requested permission for autopsy for further medical research to assist the doctors to help future medical treatment. Her parents struggled for a long time and finally agreed begrudgingly with one special request by her mother. She wanted the doctor to use anesthetic before cutting her daughter. The mother did not want her daughter to suffer any more pain.

Of course this request seemed unnecessary because the girl's body was already cold. She could not feel any pain. But the deep love inside her mother did not change, nor did it end. She still cared about her daughter. She could still feel her daughter's pain under the knife because the love of parents will not be altered by time or condition. It lasts forever!

Parents are a symbol of our Creator's love. The Creator entrusts parents as angels of love to look after children. They use unchangeable love to raise children. Parents always try to give their children the best. There are divorced mates but parents never divorce their relationship with children. Your parents may not be as educated as you are and they may not be as capable as you are. However, they have more experience than you. Don't you think that their experience, wisdom and tender love are precious to you?

20

Advice to parents

Allow me to say to parents a few words, which adolescents should also know.

The best gift God gives to parents is their children. On this world you cannot find another child like yours. Your child is created by God in His image and given birth through you. Therefore, he/she has God's image and your appearance, personality, and temperament. God entrusts the most beautiful child in your hands. "Sons are heritage from the Lord." (Psalms 127:3) If your child is a heritage, you should not possess him/her. Parents are only guardians! Using God's given love and life we as parents make every good effort to raise the most precious and unique person from God.

We must show our respect for our adolescents through our actions — give them more freedom; treat them as friends, allow them to grow up with us, the imperfect parents. We should not use authoritative pressure to treat them. Instead, together we learn to find the right direction through trials and errors.

Dear parents, the following are some suggestions to help raise your adolescents:

1. Treat them as friends.

We must show our respect to our children through actions. Allow them to exercise their free-will; give them more freedom to do things they wants; and support them as if they were little children. Gradually they will know more than we know. Their knowledge will be broader than ours. Parents are no longer the commanders-in-chief who set out orders. We can gain knowledge and experience from our adolescents.

2. Do not use high pressure.

If we are friends of adolescents, aside from adhering to our principles, we should allow open discussion regarding various aspects of life. If conflict arises during discussion, we can give them suggestions. If suggestions are not accepted, we can try to solve the problem with dignity. In case nothing works and the discussed problem is endangering your adolescent, you can enlist the help of your child's trusted friend, adult, or counselor. Often adolescents are more willing to listen to the third party than to parents whom adolescents consider old fashioned. Applying pressure is like playing with a ball, the harder the pressure, the higher the ball bounces. It only achieves the opposite result.

3. Grow with them.

Every adult has gone through the difficult phase of adolescence. Your adolescents will be forever grateful if you understand, accept, support, and tolerate them during this stormy period of life. Let them know that you had experienced similar adversities and headaches. (It is comforting to know that their experience is not unique.)

Adolescence is a period between childhood and adulthood. It is a period when adolescents are tired of childhood yet unsure of their future. They want to become adults but still have some childish behavior and thinking. This emotional disharmony is most prominent between the ages of 13 and 16 when their adolescent demeanor troubles parents. While adolescents' emotions are still unstable, they have so much exterior pressure and challenge to face. They naturally are filled with anxiety while they try to develop their self-images and value standard. Anger, withdrawal, self-pity, hostility, and depression are all byproducts of this passing phase. Parents and family members are natural targets for these emotions.

Adolescents are often misunderstood and reprimanded by parents. Very few adolescents pass through this period unscathed — actually both most adolescents and parents suffer immensely. Some parents do not wish to lose their status as parents. Some parents are reluctant to let their children grow up. Some parents worry that their children are unable to cope outside the house. Consequently, instead of helping their children become independent and mature emotionally; these parents create hurt, anxiety, and bitterness in their children. Therefore, parents should read books or take classes about adolescents. Set yourself up as models and grow together with your adolescents.

4. Encourage your adolescents to join church.

Encourage your adolescents to partake in normal church life and join youth activities, where they will meet friends of both sexes. In that setting, they will learn many aspects of human relations, such as understanding, cooperation, and making friends. They can spend some time in each other's house to learn independence. You can be worry free without being with them.

In addition, a church counselor can guide them through some of the essential problems during adolescence. Once their spiritual void is filled with God's words, their whole lives will be on the right path. Parents should also join the church themselves in order to understand their adolescents' activities. By doing so you and your adolescents can grow together in a loving environment. In a church, adolescents will learn independence while treating parents' love and opinions with respect and appreciation. A church is a big loving family, which is ideal for both parents and children to grow together.

5. Do not be a dictator.

If parents use authoritarian methods to disciple, their children will likely be rebellious. They may appear subdued by your authority; but deep down they will be averse to your teaching. "Discipline" and "teaching" include supervising and guiding. It is not right to raise children by reprimand and punishment alone. Remember to set yourselves up as models for them to emulate. Guide them with God's words. Use proper manners and words to show your care and love. Applying pressure will only achieve negative results.

6. Control your moods.

When dealing with your adolescent's problem, remain calm particularly if you have had a bad day at work or some other worries. Otherwise, your judgment and guidance could be inaccurate and you end up confusing your child.

7. Display your sincerity.

If parents sincerely want to communicate, most adolescents are happy to comply. Unfortunately, some parents lack the sincerity — they display poor attitude; impatience; and look down up children's views. Naturally this type of parents will turn children off. At times some parents are too busy to listen carefully or rashly cut off their conversation before children can finish what they want to say. "That's enough!" or "You are too young to know anything!" or "It's useless!" or "If you fail your grade again, you will have to move out." All too often parents show authority instead of sympathy or encouragement to their adolescents.

8. Do not insist on your opinion.

Some people in their tendency to maintain their "high position" will become opinionated and quick to jump to conclusion. They get mad and even slap their children. They recount children's past mistakes. Of course under this circumstance, there will not be any good communication and children will be afraid to show their feelings. Some parents place unreasonable expectations on their children, creating a great of pressure. When adolescents fall short of parents' expectation, they will distance themselves.

9. Do not compare with others.

Parents must not compare other children with their own. Do not say "So and so is such a good kid." Do not give negative comments, which only damage a child's ego. "You will never change." "Next door so-and-so is better than you." " I know you are useless. Why do I raise you?" This is one of the most damaging ways to destroy your child's self-confidence. Your opinions are really matters to them. Be careful of what you say!

10. Do not use your relationship as a weapon.

Avoid using the following expression: "If you love your mother, do..." "If you respect your parents, do not make friends of bad character." "You will be my good child if you study medicine or law." "If you want to marry that girl, we will sever our relationship." "You are trying to give me a heart attack, right?" This is manipulation. It never works in the long run.

11. Give appropriate praises.

Giving your children appropriate praise, affirmation, and appreciation as well as being proud of their achievement are the best medicine for their emotional health and incentive for working harder. Chinese parents are not good in this area. They normally give criticism, not praise. Accordingly, adolescents feel they never measure up to their parents; they are forever failures; they can never do anything to make their parents happy. They need to hear your words of praise.

12. Be a model.

Give your children physical, emotional, and spiritual education. Start with yourself. Then encourage your children to do it. Some parents encourage adolescents to join church activities or attend church services. But they themselves turn around and worship other idols. These double standards will cause adolescents to lose respect for their parents.

13. Give unconditional love.

Actively promote good relations with your children. Love them with unconditional love. This unconditional love comes form God. Human love is often conditional, unlike God's unconditional love. Sometimes it is difficult to love our children when they are bad, disobedient, or rebellious. Only when God's love touches us can we use God's love to touch our children's heart.

14. Invest your time.

Whenever possible, have a date with your adolescents. Invite them to dine out. Letting them choose their favorite restaurant and favorite food will show that you respect they choices. If timing is right, tell them of your past adversities (or failures) and how you had overcome them.

If you have time, play ball, chess, or go shopping with them. Invite their friends to come to your house and make friends with your adolescents' friends. Spending time with adolescents is a good investment. You will leave your adolescents with fond memories and enhance your relationship. Support them at sports by attending their games. This is extremely important to show your child you are interested in what he/she does.

15. Give them dignity.

Never criticize your adolescents in front of other people. Lest you make them lose face and want to hide in a hole and they will not want to go out with you whenever there are people. On the contrary, if you praise them accept them appropriately in front of others; they will feel that parents are like friends. They will be able to build healthy self-esteem and self-image. They will enjoy spending time with you.

TEACHING FROM THE BIBLE

Perhaps some of you parents say to me, "Your advice makes sense. But you do not understand my pain inflicted by my own adolescents. The pain was so unbearable that I am about to give them up." Yes, I do know your feelings. I would like to use two stories in the Bible as food for thought.

The first story is found in the Gospel of John 11:38-44. Jesus went to visit his friend's grave four days after he died. Jesus looked up and prayed. Then he called in a loud voice, "Lazarus, come out!" The dead man came out, his hands and feet wrapped with strips of linen, and a cloth around his face. Jesus said to them, "Take off the grave clothes and let him go." In this miracle, Jesus used constructive words to raise Lazarus form the dead. But he did not use the same power to take off the grave clothes form Lazarus. He turned around to the surrounding people and said, "Take off the grave clothes and let him go." This reveals to us that God has the power to give life. However, He wants to use man (you) to give others free life.

God created your child. He gives life to your child. However, your child does not have a lot of free space. Just like Lazarus, your child is bound by layers of grave clothes (agonizing feelings, unhealed bad memory, suppressed pain, etc). When we become parents God reveals to us that we need to serve our child. He also tells us to, "Take off the grave clothes and let him go."

The second story is recorded in Genesis chapter 50. Joseph was sold by his bothers as a slave in foreign country, Egypt. After many years of hardship and adversities, he became the prime minister of Egypt. The original intention of Joseph's brothers was to harm him. Little did they know that because of that intension Joseph's life was completely turned around and he was able to save his whole family. Joseph said to his brother, "You intended to harm me, but God intended it for good to accomplish what is now being done, the saving of many lives." (Genesis 50:20)

Dear parents, do you want to be God's partners? I would like to remind adolescents as well as parents that youngsters during adolescence firmly believe "Now is forever." They think the current condition will never change. They think that the present condition will last a whole life. For instance, if an adolescent has an inferiority complex and is not well liked, he thinks that nobody will ever like him. The truth is just the opposite. Adolescence is just a fleeting period. It will leave you with vague memories. It is like the clouds in the sky — same pattern will never appear twice. Some parents have a pessimistic outlook of their child. They think all is hopeless. Nonetheless, whatever weird conduct an adolescent displays, it is only a byproduct of an interim period. As long as you use love, patience, and faith to guide him and caution him, all the bad behaviors will be corrected. He will learn his hard lesson. All growing needs time. The current situation will change — it will become normal. The conflicts, worries, and hardship during adolescence will pass by like time. What awaits you is a new world with your grown child in it.

Please bear in mind "Never, never forget that Jesus loves you." He understands your need and desire. When you are happy, He shares your happiness. When you are sad and crying, He shares your sorrow. He will wipe your tears away. He is a compassionate God. Just like King David who says, "Even though I walk through the valley of the shadow of death, I will fear no evil, for you are with me, your rod and you staff, they comfort me." (Psalm 23:4)

Reference

1. American Academy of Pediatrics. *Substances Abuse: A Guide For Health Professionals.* Il. USA: American Academy of Pediatrics/Pacific Institute fro Research and Evaluation, 1988.

2. Anderson, Christy, & Wes Black. *Self-Image.* Group Paper, USA: 1995.

3. De Moss, Robert. Jr. *A Generation at Risk.* Colorado Spring, USA: focus on the family, 1993.

4. Dobson, James. *Raising Teenagers, Pocket Guides.* Il. USA: Tyndale House Publishers Inc. 1988.

5. Dobson, James. *Preparing for Adolescence.* Colorado Spring, USA: Regal Books, 1989.

6. Dobson, James. *Advice to Pre-Teenagers About Self-Confidence.* Colorado Spring, USA: focus on the family, 1992.

7. Dobson, James. *Questions Parents Ask About Self-esteem.* Colorado Spring, USA: focus on the family, 1992.

8. Dobson, James. *Self-Esteem For Your Child.* Colorado Spring, USA: focus on the family, 1993.

9. Dobson, James. *Self-Esteem Among Adults.* Colorado Spring, USA: focus on the family, 1993.

10. Goldstein, Arnold P. *Delinquents on Delinquency.* Il. USA: Research Press, 1990.

11. Kaplan. Harold I. & Benjamin J. Sadock. *Concise Textbook of Clinical Psychiatry.* Baltimore, USA: Williams & Wilkins, 1996.

12. Kliegman, Behrman, & Nelson Awin. *Textbook of Pediatrics.* Philadelphia, USA: J.B. Lippincott Company, 2000.

13. Oski, Frank A. *Principles and Practice of Pediatrics.* Philadelphia, USA: J.B. Lippincott Company, 1994.

14. Ratcliff, Donald. *Handbook of Preschool Religious Education.* Alabama, USA: Religious Education Press, 1988.

15. Ratcliff, Donald. *Handbook of Children's Religious Education*. Alabama, USA: Religious Education Press, 1988.

16. Reisser, Paul C. *Complete Book of Baby & Child Care*. IL. USA: TyndaleHouse Publisher Inc., 1997.

17. Ross, Richard, & Judi Hayes. *Ministry With Youth In Crisis*. Tennessee, USA: Convention Press, 1988.

18. Smith, Barton D. *Your Child's Health*. New York, USA: Bantam Books, 1991.

19. Strommen, Merton P. *Five Cries of Youth*. New York, USA: Harper San Francisco, 1993.

20. Watson, E.H. & G.H. Lowrey. *Growth and Development of Children*. Chicago, USA: Year Book Medical Publishers Inc., 1951.

21. Weston, William L. & Alfred T. Lane. *Color Textbook of Pediatric Dermatology*. St. Louis, USA: Mosby Year Book, 1991.

22. W. Luke Huang. *Where There Is Love, There Is Sheep - A personal Evangelicalism & Nurturing Handbook*. LA, USA: EFCCC, 2001.

23. W. Luke Huang. *Different Aspect of Teenage*. Taipei, Taiwan: Chinese Christian Medical Mission, 1997.

24. Wilfred Su. *The Magnificent Christian Family*. LA, USA: EFCCC, 1995.

25. *Focus on Chinese Family: Volume 2:No.5, 6, 8, & 9, 1997*, LA, USA: Focus on Chinese Family, 1997.

26. Chinese Daily News, (2002, Feb.27). *Teens Drinking*, pA5.

27. Roger Peter D. & Werner Mark J. *Substance abuse — the pediatric Clinics of North America*. USA: W.B. Saunders Company, 1995.

Book Title:	**Growth of Adolescence:** A Guide for Teens and Parents
Authors:	**W. Luke Huang,** M.D., MBA
Publisher:	**EFC-Communication Center**
	9386 Telstar Ave.
	El Monte, CA 91731, U.S.A.
	Tel: (626) 307-0030
	Fax: (626) 307-5557
	Ordering Line: (800) 888-7796
Editors:	**Janet Hsu, Lily Huang**
First Edition:	June, 2002
	Printed in U.S.A.
	All Right Reserved
	ISBN 1-885216-40-8